Living in Grace

KENNON L. CALLAHAN, PH.D.

Wherever we find grace,
we find compassion, peace, and hope.
These four are good friends.

For additional copies of *Living in Grace,* you are welcome to visit the following link: www.createspace.com/4086926

ISBN: 1-4812-0088-7

ISBN-13: 978-1-4812-0088-2

Library of Congress Control Number: 2012923444

CreateSpace Independent Publishing Platform

North Charleston, SC

Table of Contents

II WAYS TO STUDY AND APPLY THE LEARNINGS

III THE BLESSING

IV AUTHOR, BOOKS, APPRECIATION

Dedication

Herbert Hoffman

Herbert Hoffman was a most extraordinary person. His gifts of ministry, music, shepherding, and leadership have blessed many persons. He had an extraordinary mind and a wonderful thoughtfulness with people.

For years, he was among the most outstanding ministers of music in the United States. His grace and thoughtfulness, his gifted musical ability and warm spirit, and his inspiring direction brought out the best in choirs of all ages.

In later years, he served with distinction as minister of planning and administration for several major congregations. His gifts of helping people to move forward in mission have had a profound influence. His encouraging leadership has been remarkable. He has made significant contributions in the lives of many persons.

Herbert Paul Hoffman, 1928–2008, was the first of three children born in Youngstown, Ohio, to Lucile and Paul Hoffman. Herb was educated at Youngstown University, Westminister Choir College, and Wayne State University's Institute of Music, graduating with a diploma in conducting and voice.

His entire life was devoted to the Church.

Herb and Doris Jean Ross Burley were married on October 14, 1967, and shared many happy years of married life together. Their common love of music was a wondrous gift to many persons and congregations across the years.

For the first thirty-two years of his ministry, he served as minister of music for churches across the country with memberships from 800 to 4,000. These congregations included Pontiac and Ferndale, Michigan; First Methodist Church, Cuyahoga Falls, Ohio; Phoenix, Arizona; Athens, Georgia; Johnson City, Tennessee; and Abilene, Texas.

For the last twenty years of his ministry, he served as minister of programs, administration, evangelism, and lay ministries in Albuquerque, New Mexico, and Centreville, Virginia. He was consecrated as a diaconal minister in 1977, retired in 1999, and continued to work for two years after that. In his retired years, he was an active leader in St. John's United Methodist Church of Aiken, South Carolina.

Herbert Paul Hoffman was a person of grace, compassion, community, and hope. His gifts of grace and wisdom blessed the lives of many, many persons. He is among the remarkable persons we will ever know.

Foreword

Living in Grace is a joyful, encouraging book. It shares
encouraging possibilities to live life in the grace of God. In this
new book you will discover twelve decisive events.
Each event will strengthen your understanding of grace.

I am grateful to all of the persons who have
participated in these events. All of the persons have
a special place in my heart. They have been helpful in my life
and in the lives of many persons across the years.

As you read each chapter you will discover these extraordinary
persons. They will become new, good friends in your life. These
persons have given much to my way of living and loving, thinking
and doing. I am most grateful. All of them have contributed key
learnings of discovering and living in grace. I thank all of them.

I share these events and these good friends with you in the
hope that both your experiencing and understanding of God's
grace will bless and encourage, deepen, and enlarge your life.
May you live a joyful life in grace.

I am thankful to Doris Hoffman, Sara Huron, Richard
Worden, and Leo Bardes for their contributions in the writing
of this book. Each of them has given of their special gifts and
competencies to advance *Living in Grace*. This has become a
most helpful, encouraging, and valuable book because of their
contributions. I am grateful we share this life together as good
friends, colleagues, and family.

I am grateful to the CreateSpace team of Chris, Andrea, Ashley, Karen, Colleen, Molly, and Gaines. This is an impressive staff of persons. I have enjoyed our work together and our work on this book has flowed remarkably well. It has been a joy to work with them. Of course, I take full responsibility for the final book.

Many, many persons – the people who participated in these twelve events, the special reader team who helped me with the book, and the publisher's staff - bring this book to you.

May you enjoy and benefit from *Living in Grace*.

Living in Grace is a joyful, encouraging, and helpful way to live life. Welcome to grace. Welcome to life. Welcome to the encouraging spirit in this book.

Kennon L. Callahan, Ph.D.

I

Twelve Key Events

Decisive Events

GRACE-FILLED EVENTS

Decisive events change our lives and shape our destinies. This is a book of decisive events that have changed my life and shaped my destiny. Events are decisive when they are filled with grace. Grace-filled events change our lives and shape our destinies.

Our lives are filled with every day, ordinary events. We live and move and have our being amidst the routine, regular events of life. We awake. We rise. We get ready. We go to work. We tend to matters around the house. We have meals. We visit and share with one another. We laugh. We cry. We worry. We wonder. We are glad. We are sad. We play. We love. We go to sleep. We waken. We rise.

We live day to day, week to week, month to month, year to year, hardly noticing as the years come and go. We experience events, we experience people, we remember old friends, we make new friends, we practice old habits, we discover new possibilities, we accomplish much, and we spend and waste time as though we had a million years.

Amidst the every day, ordinary events of life, we experience decisive events that change our lives and shape our destinies. We experience the grace of God in these events. Our learnings for living come from these decisive, grace-filled events.

LEARNINGS

I call these *learnings*. They are more than lessons. The term *lessons* has a fixed, static sense. It is as though a lesson is once learned, and is now a fixed part of one's makeup. A lesson is something that has happened, and, then, we move on. Life is more dynamic than that.

A learning is something we experience each day, new and fresh. Each day, with newfound wonder and deep, amazing joy, we learn, we discover anew, the learning that has come to us in some event that has happened in our lives. We discover new possibilities, new feelings, new meanings, and new ways forward. The decisive event continues to change our life and shape our destiny.

This monograph includes twelve learnings that have come to me. These twelve events, and the persons who participated in them, tell a remarkable story of wonderful discoveries for life. I am grateful to have been a part of these events. They have been decisive for me and for the direction of my own life.

These twelve events are shared just as they happened.

They have not been embellished. There is no need to add to or exaggerate. Yes, I have changed some of the names of the persons involved in these events. But I have not added to the events.

These events are remarkable in themselves. It is sufficient to share the events simply as they happened. From Julie to Bobby to John and Mary—for all twelve events, I share them as they happened.

From time to time, persons and groups have encouraged me to write my autobiography. They want to know more of what has formed and shaped my unique perspective that has led to the publication of my books – nineteen at recent count. The books travel the planet and have lives of their own.

As a way forward, I have felt led to share these twelve events in my life.

These events have been decisive for developing my way of thinking, encouraging, consulting, and teaching. These events have helped to shape my way of living and loving, my understanding and theology. These twelve events continue to shape my way of living.

I have shared these twelve events, across the years, in seminars and consultations and conversations. People, again and again, have told me that these events have been most helpful. Indeed, with considerable delight, people teach me that these events help the insights and material I share to come alive.

These events have shaped me, and many of the persons, groupings, and communities with whom I have shared. We have found new discoveries, strengths, and possibilities from these events. You are welcome to enjoy these events and discover the learnings that will help you live in the grace of God.

As you read each of these twelve events, think of events in your life....

of compassion....

of strengths....

of fun, with joy and wonder....

Live your compassion. Claim your strengths. Have fun. Live with the joy and the wonder of life. Experience the grace of God.

Where life abounds, grace abounds. Where grace abounds, life abounds. In these twelve events, in these twelve learnings, the grace of God abounds.

1. LIVE YOUR COMPASSION

Julie

We live our compassion.
We live in the grace of God.

The most decisive event for me has been coming to know Julie.

We met in high school. I can see her now, sitting in the front row near the teacher's desk. Mr. Heinz presided over the third floor study hall, in room 302. He was the speech and drama teacher. With a senatorial voice, gray hair, tall of stature, a quiet spirit, and a commanding presence, he served as coach of the varsity debate team and advisor to the drama club.

My study hall was on the second floor, in room 201. I was a senior that year, which had its privileges. I was on the varsity debate team. Jim Coleman and I were partners. Jim was a grand partner. We balanced one another with our debating strengths. Together, we were an excellent match. We did well that year. We were the affirmative team, and we won many debates against major competition. It was an extraordinary year.

During the course of the year, I would get a hall pass to go from my study hall to Mr. Heinz's study hall. He and I would discuss strategies for the upcoming debate tournaments. It was especially useful preparation for the coming Saturday debates.

Julie and I came to know one another. She was a sophomore. Sitting near Mr. Heinz's desk gave us the opportunity to visit. She is a generous person, with a spirit of confidence and assurance, openness and graciousness. We would talk, particularly on those occasions when Mr. Heinz had to run an errand and left me in charge of the study hall. Julie and I became friends.

On January 30, 1954, a decisive event changed my life and shaped my destiny. It was a grace-filled, compassion-filled event.

In any month that had five Saturdays, Julie's church would schedule a square dance. Julie invited me. We had our first date. We had a wonderful time. We dated again. More dates followed. As I came to know her better, I discovered, increasingly, her quiet, gentle ways of sharing compassion with those around her. We fell in love.

In the spring of her junior year, Julie gave me her junior picture. On the back, she wrote:

Ken,

I'll never forget that first time we went out together. Remember—I had asked you to that square dance at church?

We've certainly had some wonderful times since then, haven't we?
Let's not let them stop now but just keep right on having fun together.

All my love to a really wonderful guy.

Julie

We continued to date. We went steady.

The next year, in her senior year, in the spring, Julie gave me her senior picture. On the back, she wrote:

Ken,

I've found in you alone a friend who's been worth knowing;
And as the years pass us by, our friendship keeps on growing.

You are someone I will always hold dear.
To you I've always taken every joy and every fear.

You've always been a comfort when I felt I had no friend.
Your kindness and your love seem never to know an end.

This seems to be the only way that I ever can express
The love your friendship gives me and all the happiness!

Love,

Julie

We became engaged. Time passed. We married.

On January 29, 2012, Julie and I celebrated the fifty-eighth anniversary of our first date. Then, on August 11, 2012, we celebrated the fifty-sixth anniversary of our marriage.

Julie is the most remarkable person I know. Her compassion and wisdom, her kindness and gentle spirit bless my life and the lives of many. We share a rich, full life together. We celebrate many wonderful years of married life together.

Two excellent sons have been born to us. They are gifts of God. They have emerged as solid human beings. We are proud to be their parents. Three grandchildren bless our lives. We are grateful for these years together, and for our two sons, Ken and Mike, our daughter-in-law, Shay, and our three grandsons, Blake, Mason, and Brice.

We celebrate many remarkable years of ministry together. We began serving as associate minister of a congregation while studying at the university. It was an amazing time, sharing with hardworking people. Mostly, they were employed in the nearby tire factories of Akron, Ohio.

We lived on the third floor of the Wesley Foundation at Kent State University and looked after the building. Rev. Bill Van Valkenburg was the director. He was an immense encouragement and a generous friend. During this time, we also served the Mountville and Thompson congregations, while their pastor was on an extended leave.

Then, we were the first pastoral couple actually to live in Brady Lake. The sign said Brady Lake Community Church. They arranged with the district superintendent to have a pastor preach. Prior to our coming, once a month or sometimes once a week, a pastor would drive out to Brady Lake to preach on Sunday.

The year we went to Brady Lake, there was no parsonage. We lived that summer with Mrs. Ida Mae Stratton in her big, old farmhouse. Her husband had died that spring. She had room. We would be company with her. We had a grand time sharing and living together. Her strawberry patch was right outside her kitchen door. Each evening we would have strawberries for dessert.

In the fall, a small cottage was found down on the lake. It was for rent. It would work well. Living catty-corner across the lane from us were Orville and Mary Hissom. Big, warm, wise Orville was the principal of the school and mentor of the community. We learned much from him. Mary was cheerful, with a sense of joy in her life. She was a nurse, and when later our first son was born, she was a wonderful help to us.

Harold and Wilma Dodds lived two houses down from us, right across from the Hissoms. Harold had a good spirit and practical common sense, and he could fix almost anything. Wilma shared the warmth of her happiness, her humor, and her tender ways.

They and the Hissoms were close, good friends. The four of them were generous to include us and to love us, warmly and fully. Many an evening, we sat together on the Dodds' front porch, our laughter floating out across the lake, sharing with one another, talking of family, reflecting on life and its course.

These were good friends and good times. During our time at Brady Lake, we— meaning the congregation, with much volunteer labor—built a parsonage, which has helped the community to have a pastor ever since.

In the years that have come and gone, Julie and I have had the privilege of serving congregations in Ohio, Texas, and Georgia. We share our gratitude with the people of Goodyear Heights, Mountville, Thompson, Brady Lake, Lovers Lane, Pleasant Valley, Bethel, Mt. Gilead, Turin, and Coke's Chapel. We have learned much from them and their compassion.

We have spoken to countless seminars; workshops; and regional, national, and international events. We have had the privilege of helping thousands of key leaders and ministers. We have traveled afar. We have served as consultants with thousands of congregations, helping them develop a strong, healthy future in God's mission.

We have had the honor of teaching for many years at one of the strongest seminaries on the planet. We have taught, shared with, and learned from thousands of students who are now serving God's mission in extraordinary ways.

The books we have written have a life of their own. They travel around the globe, benefiting people in this country,

Canada, England, Korea, South Africa, Australia, New Zealand, and beyond. Translated into various languages, they are used in Korea, a number of countries in Africa, the Caribbean, Latvia, Austria, Russia, and nations in Central and South America.

We share many remarkable years of marriage and ministry. We look forward to the years to come, and the ways in which we can best serve God's mission. In each place we have lived, Julie has shared her compassion—with children in the neighborhood, people in the hospital, with her colleagues at work, individuals in need, and with her family.

God's greatest gift to me is, finally, not the congregations served, students helped, courses taught, seminars led, lectures delivered, national and international events spoken to, the honors and awards bestowed, or the churches strengthened with my consultation. Nor is it the books written, translated, and used around the world. These are remarkable gifts, given of God.

Yet they pale compared to God's primary gift to me. If I could be known for anything, it would not be for these things.

God's greatest gift to me is to be "Julie's husband." In the area of the Rocky Mountains where we like to spend much of our free time, Julie is known widely for her contributions in several groups, especially in the quilting group. This is among the strongest groups in the region. With my speaking and travel schedule, she is there more than I am. She is better known there than I am. When I meet someone in the area for the first time, the person says, with considerable joy, delight, and enthusiasm, "You're Julie's husband!" To be Julie's husband is the deepest, richest honor in this life's journey.

Late one night as I was writing, these words came to me.

Intelligent and wise
Gentle and soft
A star in her eyes
She saw the future before I did

A wonderful surprise
The path we have followed
Is more than I could dream
The wonder of it all
Is hers to glean

Hope is life
Hope is my wife
Love is life
Love is my wife . . . . Julie

God blesses us with people with whom we discover the full meaning of compassion. I am grateful for the countless mentors and friends whom God has given to me, and who have shared and now share their compassion with me. I have discovered much about compassion through the grace of God, the compassion of Christ, and the hope of the Holy Spirit.

I am especially grateful for all I have learned and am discovering about compassion from Julia Ross McCoy Callahan. God sends special people to each of us. I am thankful God sent Julie to me. Her compassion and wisdom, her sense of generosity, her gentle sharing with people, her deep love for people, her sense of forgiveness, generous and full—all these help me understand the richness, the fullness of compassion.

LIVE YOUR COMPASSION

Live your compassion. You will live in the grace of God.

When you live your compassion, you live a life full of joy and wonder, good fun and good times, forgiveness, reconciliation, and moving on. When you live with compassion, you claim God's gift of compassion for you. Whatever depth of compassion you share, you share because you have discovered the depth of God's compassion for you. When you live a life of your compassion, you share the compassion of God with yourself and those around you.

When you deny your compassion, you deny God's gift of compassion in your life. You deny God. Some people live half their lives, preoccupied with themselves, resentful and bitter, selfish and defensive, holding grudges, and unforgiving of people who have wronged them and abused them. They deny God's gift of compassion. They deny God.

God gives each of us loved ones, like Julie, and mentors, coaches, and encouragers with whom we discover the compassion of God. God comes to us directly, with amazing compassion. God comes to us in Christ, surrounding us with compassion. God comes to us as Holy Spirit, leading us forward with compassion.

And, God sends to us persons like Julie, and mentors, coaches, and encouragers so we will experience compassion in our lives. As we experience the gift of compassion, we are able to share the richness of compassion with those around us.

Think with your heart. Live with your heart. Enjoy life with your heart. Trust your heart. People become married out of compassion, not reasonability. If it made reasonable sense, most people would not be married. People marry because of their love for one another, not because it makes sense. Then, they rationalize why it makes sense to get married earlier rather than later.

Christ dies on the cross, not because it makes sense, but because he loves us. Wesley came down from that upper room describing his heart as strangely warmed, not precisely logical. We do what we do, mostly with love and compassion for the people God gives to us. Much of everything done in humankind is done on compassion.

Of a morning, when you first arise, live your compassion. It is not that you share your compassion once, and then move on in living your life. Things will come up. Grudge and guilt will try to find you. Egoism and selfishness will seek to be your friends. Hurt feelings and resentments will try to distract you. Self-centeredness will quietly slip back in.

For a whole, healthy life, it is helpful that you live, *this day,* the compassion with which you are blessed.

As you live your compassion, you will include new persons with whom you share compassion. As you live your compassion, you confirm God's gift of compassion in your life. As you live your compassion, you begin *this day* with God. It is more fun to begin your day with God than without God. Live your compassion. Live, *this day,* in the grace of God.

Where there is compassion, there is the grace of God.

Prayer

Almighty and Everliving God, we are grateful for your compassion in our lives. We are amazed at the wonder of your love for us. We are thankful for the decisive acts of compassion with which you bless our lives. Forgive us, we pray, when we are less than grateful. Help us to grow forward to the lives of compassion you encourage us to live.

With the grace of God, we pray.

Amen.

2. CLAIM YOUR STRENGTHS

Bobby

We claim our strengths.
We live in the grace of God.

A most decisive event in my own life is a baseball game. The most decisive person in the game is Bobby.

It was the ninth inning. We had "last bats." We were three runs behind. There were two outs against us. We had no one on base. We were playing late that Saturday night for the citywide championship. We were sort of sitting, glum and gloomy, kicking our cleats into the dirt of the dugout, waiting for the inevitable end.

The championship we had worked so hard for all season was slowly slipping from our grasp. Even our people in the stands were packing up, getting ready to leave, gathering up their things, to beat the rush.

Our next batter hit a single and made it to first. A little titter of excitement in the dugout. Not much in the stands—still packing. Our next batter had the good sense to stand there and do nothing. He got a walk. We now had two men on base—first and second. There was a little more excitement in the dugout. Still, it was the bottom of the ninth, two outs. Mostly our people in the stands were still packing. A few were beginning to wonder whether to stay and see what might happen.

Our next batter hit a blazing grounder to the shortstop, who bobbled the ball and before he could make the forced play at second that would win the citywide championship, our man had gotten there, so he threw to first. The throw was late.

We now had the bases loaded! Two outs, bottom of the ninth, three runs behind. The citywide championship was once again within our grasp!

The excitement, the cheers, the carrying-on, the hugging, the back-slapping—more injuries occur at this point in a game than any other—and the shouting happening in the dugout were all amazing to behold. Our people in the stands had decided it was worth staying. They were on their feet, cheering to the high heavens. We now had the chance, once again, to be citywide champions.

Amidst all this hullabaloo and carrying on, Bobby—the batter on deck—had gone faithfully and dutifully to the plate, to do his dead-level best for the team.

When my guys saw who was now standing in the batter's box with the citywide championship resting on the line, the words they shared with their beloved coach—namely me—are words I cannot share in this good company. Bobby had successfully struck out every time he went to bat across the whole season.

Quick background.

Bobby's father had come to me at the beginning of the season. He had said to me,

"We had our son late in life. We were in our forties when he was born. He has mostly grown up among adults. We may have played catch a couple of times in the backyard. He has never owned a glove, a ball, or a bat. He has never been on a team. We think it would be helpful to Bobby's development if he could just practice with your team.

"We wouldn't expect him to play in the game. We know the record your team has had in previous seasons. Maybe during the game, he could serve as batboy, or water boy, or something. We would deeply appreciate it if he could simply practice with your team. We think it would help him."

I said to Bobby's father, "I have a problem. My philosophy, my policy, is whoever comes to practice plays. What you can count on and depend on is when Bobby comes to practice, he will play. I'll try to see that he doesn't get into a spot where he is over his head."

Those last words were turning out to be prophetic, fateful words; he was clearly over his head late that Saturday night.

Bobby, you see, was a sucker for high, outside pitches. Everybody in the league knew it. Their best pitcher knew it, and you could see the gleam in his eye. Bobby had done nothing all season. Bobby would do nothing tonight. The championship was now theirs for the taking.

Sometimes, coaches make interesting decisions. I thought about our season as a team. I looked to the stands and saw two parents, fearful, anxious, worried, not certain they really wanted their son to be standing at that point in the galaxies he was currently occupying.

I said to myself, and then to the team, "We've come through the season together as a team. We will finish the season as a team. Bobby stays."

The words that greeted that announcement are words I cannot share in this good company either. I learned new words I had not heard before. What does that word mean? I had never heard that word before. The team's loud complaining dwindled to a lesser mumbling and finally ground to a depressed silence. They knew the citywide championship was lost.

First pitch: high, outside, wild swing, strike one. You could hear the groans in the dugout.

Second pitch: high, outside, wild swing, strike two. You could see our people in the stands again packing up.

Third pitch: high, outside, no swing. Bobby was tired from the first two swings. The bat stayed on his shoulder. Ball one.

Fourth pitch: high, outside, wild swing.

The best way to describe what happened is—the ball hit the bat! With just enough force that, in a peculiar kind of blooper way, it sailed just high enough over the first baseman's outstretched glove so that he couldn't reach it. It landed fair, and with a crazy kind of spin, bounced foul.

Night game, lights on, still there are shadows. The first baseman turns, hunting and searching for the ball, knowing the game is at hand.

My guys are running! I had had the hit-and-run on for every one of those high, outside pitches. They had big leads off the bases. They were moving. The man from third was virtually sliding home. The man from second was headed to third. The man from first was almost to second.

Everyone was running, except for one person—Bobby—who was still standing at home plate.

My guys encouraged Bobby, helping him to know where he needed to be next. With a kind of dazed expression on his face, Bobby headed for a new stage in life—namely, first base. He had never been there before. As Bobby was moving to first, the man from third made it home. One run scored. The man from second rounded third, heading home.

The pitcher had made the fatal mistake of the evening. Bobby had done nothing all season. Bobby would do nothing tonight. So the pitcher had stayed on the mound, waiting to receive the cheers and accolades of the crowd for winning the championship. Normally, he would have moved over to cover first base, but now there was no one covering first base.

By the time the first baseman found the ball, Bobby was near enough first base that the first baseman saw Bobby would make it, so he did the next best thing he knew how to do. The man from second had rounded third, headed toward home. The first baseman threw home to force that out. With the confusion of the moment, he hurried his throw, threw high, and the ball went into the backstop cage. Our second run scored.

While the catcher was chasing the ball, Bobby rounded first, heading toward second. The only way the catcher could see to win the game now was to try to throw out the man who had come from first and was heading into third in a diving slide. The catcher threw the ball, and for whatever reason, he threw it through the third baseman's legs, out into left field.

We've all seen this before. When things start going wrong, they begin to collapse all over the field. Mostly, it had happened with my teams. I could empathize with the other team's coach that night. By the time the left fielder got the ball, the player who had slid into third had picked himself up and made it home. Three runs had scored.

The only player still running the bases was Bobby, who was headed to second.

The left fielder threw the ball to the second baseman to cut Bobby off as he was arriving. Again, for whatever reason, the ball went high over the second baseman's glove and headed back out into right field. Bobby rounded second, getting up a head of steam.

One of the things Bobby knew how to do best was run.

Meek, quiet, shy, bashful Bobby. He had learned to run mostly through first and second and third and fourth and fifth and sixth grades and beyond, because the teasers, the tormentors, the bullies in each class would pursue him, jeer him, harass him, taunt him, and try to beat him up. So over the years, even as he was hesitant and timid, the one thing Bobby had developed as a strength, the one thing he had learned how to do well was run—mostly away from people who were chasing him. He could run faster than the wind.

His strength, his gift was his ability to run. In baseball, he did not field well. He did not bat well. He could run.

As he rounded first, headed to second, my team and our stands took up the chant,

"Run, Bobby, run!"

As he rounded second, headed to third, the chant became louder: "RUN, BOBBY, RUN!!!" Bobby ran faster.

As he rounded third, headed to home, the chant became even louder: "RUN, BOBBY, RUN!!!! RUN, BOBBY, RUN!!!!!!!"

Bobby had spent his life running *from* people. Now, Bobby was running *for* the team who had stuck with him through the season. It was a new experience for him!

With a full head of steam, running faster than he had ever run before, Bobby headed for home!

The all-star catcher, with a sly grin on his face, waited for Bobby. The catcher, in football season, played right guard on the varsity football team. Tall, humongous, with thick weight and hard muscles, he was eager to meet Bobby.

The first baseman had found the ball. He now had his second chance to save the game, the season, the championship. He remembered what he had done the last time. You could see it in his eyes. He had hurried the throw. This time he would take his time. The last time he had thrown high. This time he would throw low.

Sure enough, the ball was slow and low. It bounced in the dirt in front of home plate. Just as it was bouncing from the dirt into the catcher's outstretched glove, Bobby lunged with all his being, so that his hand would touch the plate before the catcher could get the ball. He gathered up everything he had so he could do his overwhelming best for the team.

His hand reached the plate before the catcher had the ball!!

We were four runs to three!!!

Citywide champions!!!!

My guys did the right thing. They picked Bobby up, put him on their shoulders, and carried him all around the field. He was the hero of the season. And, I saw two parents sitting in the stands, tears gently streaming down their cheeks. Their son had come of age.

He used the one strength, the one competency with which he was blessed. He used the one talent and resource he had. He used his ability to run—with all his being and with all his might—to do his best for the team.

Whether we had won the citywide championship or not, the remarkable miracle of that night was that it was a new Bobby, running faster than the wind, lunging for home plate, his hand outstretched, doing his best for the team.

You could almost see it in him, as he made the pilgrimage toward first, rounded second, headed toward third. You could see a growing confidence and assurance in his stride, an increasing strength in his step. You could see him as he headed from third toward home, gathering up all of his energy, resources, being, every fiber in him. He intended to do everything he could for the team that had stuck with him through the season of his life.

I have this confidence: God makes all things new. Something as simple as a citywide championship becomes the event in which Bobby becomes a new person. The miracle of that night was the new Bobby in the lunge to the plate. In the time, come and gone, since that extraordinary evening, he has grown in his competencies, in his relation with God, and in his strong sense of mission. And the contributions Bobby has made in his community and across this country are amazing to behold. It began that night.

I have shared the story of Bobby just the way it happened. It is one of those remarkable nights that happens once in a lifetime.

We have all been Bobby in one way or another.

This is why Bobby's story has so much appeal. Something happens. We claim our strengths. We become new persons in the grace of God.

It is amazing how God works through simple events to help people discover their best, true selves. Bobby claimed well the strength he had: running. He used it remarkably to build for himself a new life. Rather than running away, timid, bashful, shy, this was the new Bobby who ran toward that catcher—the formidable, massive, huge, all-star catcher of the season.

It was the new Bobby who lunged with all his being to do his best for the team. Even in simple events, God helps us discover our best, true selves. We become new persons. We live in grace.

CLAIM YOUR STRENGTHS

Claim your strengths. You will live in the grace of God.

When you claim your strengths, you claim God's gifts. Whatever strengths, gifts, and competencies you have, you have them as gifts of God's grace. When you claim your strengths, you claim God.

When you deny your strengths, you deny God's gifts. You deny God. Some people live half their lives, looking down on themselves, thinking more poorly of themselves than they have a right to, suffering from low self-esteem. They deny God's gifts. They deny God.

They become preoccupied with weakness, shortcomings, mistakes, and failures.

They grumble and complain, moan and lament. They allow themselves to be sidetracked, to be diverted from their real strengths. They become anxious about what they cannot do, what strengths they do not have. They miss the strengths they do have. They miss the stirring, moving, living presence of the grace of God in their lives.

Now, I am not suggesting you think better of yourself than you have a right to.

I am suggesting that you have a realistic assessment of your strengths, gifts, and competencies. See the strengths you really have. Claim your strengths. Live with confidence and assurance in the gifts with which God has blessed you.

Sometimes, we persuade ourselves or allow ourselves to be persuaded that a specific competency is one we do well. We move away from our real competency to something else. We have a good friend whose strength is as a service writer in a service center of a car dealership. He loves the work. He excels at the work.

He is so good at it that he was persuaded to become the general manager of the whole car dealership, over service, sales, advertising, administration, and accounting. After a time—and he was a decent general manager—he asked to be, once again, a service writer. He enjoys working with customers. As general manager, he worked with staff, not customers.

We have another good friend who was persuaded by her mother to be a teacher. She did. Her mother had said, "As a teacher, you will always have a job." She always did. Her real love, her real strength, was in nursing. Finally, after a time, she became a nurse. She is living out her strength and her love. She is happier than she has ever been.

A successful trial lawyer came up to me during the break of a seminar I was leading. He said, "Dr. Callahan, you are right. Five years ago, I gave up my law practice. I did it well. I helped many people. I made a great deal of money. My real strength, my real love is restoring old homes. I have been doing that for these past five years. I have never been happier. Yes, I am claiming my real strength, my real love."

There are countless people who have discovered their strengths, have claimed their strengths, and are living happy lives. God encourages you to do the same.

Of a given morning, when you first arise, claim your strengths. It is not that you claim your strengths once, and then move on in living your life. Things will come up. You will get busy. You will be sidetracked. You will long for someone else's strengths. You will begin to be preoccupied. You will begin to forget. You will develop amnesia. You will slide back. Low self-esteem will quietly slip back in.

For a whole, healthy life, it is helpful that you confirm the strengths you have.

As you develop new strengths—and you will—include them as you name your strengths. As you claim your strengths, you claim God's gifts. As you claim God's gifts, you begin *this day* with God. It is more fun to begin your day with God than without God. Claim your strengths.

Where persons claim their strengths, there is the grace of God.

Prayer

Living God, we are grateful for the strengths with which you bless our lives. When we are anxious, help us to claim our strengths. When we are fearful, lead us to our strengths. When we are doubtful, give us the peace of our strengths. Forgive us when we are envious of someone else's strengths. Help us to claim our own strengths, gifts, and competencies.

With the grace of God, we pray.

Amen.

3. HAVE FUN

Marie and Jason and the Great Banquet

We have fun.
We live in the grace of God.

Have fun. Live in the grace of God. Live happiness. When you live your compassion and when you claim your strengths, you have the gift of being able to have fun. The three are good friends: compassion, strengths, fun.

The music lifted. The congregation turned. Marie was standing in the doorway. Her father was beside her. The groom, the groomsmen, and the bridesmaids were in place. As the minister, I had gone in first. The groom, the groomsmen, and the bridesmaids had followed.

Now, the five young flower girls were ready. They began their lovely dance down the center aisle, solemn and serious, then smiling and laughing and then giggling and dancing. They were happy to be part of this wondrous event.

Marie and her father started down the aisle. The congregation rose. The music stirred. There were smiles all around. The hopes and dreams of all the years were gathered as Marie and her father came down the aisle.

Marie and Jason were getting married! The spirit of wonder and joy filled the chapel! The wedding, long anticipated, was now at hand! There was much laughter. There was much fun. And the fun and laughter continued at the wedding reception.

Indeed, the fun and laughter had begun weeks before.

Marie and Jason had planned the wedding well. For nearly a year they developed the events that would surround the wedding. The nearly a year was filled with much anticipation and merriment. Phone calls, emails, and letters were filled with excitement and gladness. England, America, Australia—people were coming from all these places.

Marie and Jason live in London. Marie's family lives in Texas. Jason's family is coming from Australia. The wedding gathers people from three continents. More phone calls, emails, and letters brighten the anticipation.

This is to be the happiest time of their lives. And it is. The gatherings before, the rehearsal, the rehearsal dinner, the wedding, the wedding reception, and more were filled with wonder and joy, laughter and good fun.

The wedding reception was a great feast, held at a grand resort. There was much laughter. There were many speeches and toasts to the bride and groom. There was music and dancing. The adults danced. The children danced. There were tears of joy and wonder. There were pictures upon pictures. The air was filled with happiness. There were more speeches and toasts. This was one of the happiest days of our lives.

The kingdom of God is like a wedding feast!

We have all been to events like this. We are filled with wonder and joy, hope and happiness. We experience these events as decisive in our lives and destinies. We experience the grace of God.

Likewise, the kingdom of God is like a great banquet!

Each family brought a dish. Some brought a dish and a dessert. The tables were filled to overflowing with foods of all kinds. It was a wonderful gathering—near Christmas. The whole congregation was gathering. There was a tree, decorated the week before by the women of the church. There were presents under the tree for the children.

Some people were setting the tables. Some were gathering the foods on the tables. Some were in the kitchen making the coffee and tea, pouring the water, bringing out the condiments of salt and pepper and other seasonings. Some people were gathered in small groups, telling the latest joke, discussing the newest news, bringing one another up to date on happenings in the community and the world.

The tables were filled with mashed potatoes and gravy, turkey and dressing. There were dishes of carrots, broccoli, and spinach. Salads and dressings graced the tables. Breads, jams, and jellies were in abundance. Lemon meringue pies, pumpkin pies, cherry pies, strawberry and rhubarb pies, and multitudes of cakes were ready for the desserts.

The children were finding one another. They love these gatherings. They chase and run. They play and laugh. They find their special toys, gathering in a corner of the room, bubbling with smiles and enthusiasm. This is among their best times. They look forward to the food, and especially to the desserts!

Gene was near the door, greeting everyone as they came in. Eileen was moving from family to family, person to person, welcoming them with her spirit of grace. Glenn was setting up the music that would help the gathering to sing with great joy and enthusiasm. Harold and Wilma were helping each person, each family, to find their places. Orville and Mary were giving special attention to persons who had had a recent disappointment or difficulty in their lives.

It was an amazing gathering.

This is not a large congregation. It is what I call a small, strong congregation. And they are large with their generosity and their love with one another. Yes, there are disagreements and disputes. There are, from time to time, heated words, best left unsaid and quickly forgiven and forgotten.

The best of families have their fair share of conflict. The only people who do not have conflict are buried in the nearest cemetery. And sometimes, when I walk by late at night, I am not so sure about them. I hear the mutterings and the murmurings. The best of families are distinguished, not by the absence of conflict, but by the presence of forgiveness, reconciliation, and moving on.

Great banquets are times for celebration, forgiveness, reconciliation, and moving on. We gather to discover and deepen our love and compassion with one another. We gather for good fun and good times. We gather for laughter and cheer, for merriment and happiness.

Great banquets are foretelling, proleptic events that anticipate and remind us of the great gatherings with loved ones and friends in the life to come. We remember and rejoice. Each gathering of grace and family stirs our memories of all the gatherings we have shared before. We discover, yet more deeply, our sense of roots, place, belonging, friends, and family. We are community. We have fun. We rejoice.

HAVE FUN

Have fun. You will live in the grace of God.

When Jesus encourages us to rejoice and to have fun he has in mind the rich, full fun of a wedding feast or a great banquet.

When I encourage us to have fun I do not mean silly fun, with its nonsensical, slaphappy spirit of ridicule. Nor do I have in mind satirical humor that pokes fun at people wherein they lose face, are embarrassed, and made to feel bad.

When Jesus is asked about the kingdom of God, he describes it as a wedding feast and a great banquet. Importantly, Christ does not describe the kingdom of God as some committee meeting or administrative report. He describes the kingdom of God as a gathering of great celebration. The kingdom of God is a great banquet of God's grace, a wedding feast of God's hope, a gathering of great happiness.

One of Coca-Cola's recent slogans is "open happiness." The picture is of a Coca-Cola bottle just being opened. The encouragement is to open the drink of happiness, to enjoy the flavor and the taste of happiness.

I encourage you to "live happiness" in the grace of God. Happiness is more than a drink. You are welcome, with the grace of God, to "open happiness, discover happiness, and live happiness." Having fun is a choice we make. Living with happiness is a choice we make. Living in the grace of God is a choice we make.

Feel free to give yourself the extraordinary gift you can give to yourself, the gift of having fun, the gift of happiness. Some people, in parting from a family member or a friend say, "Take care." Some say, "Watch out." Some say, "Look out." These are helpful sentiments and partings.

I usually say, "Have fun." My spirit is to encourage grace, happiness, and fun, in the deepest spirit for a whole, healthy life.

Some people, on rising in the morning, say to themselves, "Open sadness." They begin a new day of complaining. For whatever reasons, they have developed their "gift" for complaining and lamenting, bemoaning and whining. In Australia, it is called *whinging.* Elsewhere, it is called *mumping* or *gurning.* Some people seem bent on being grouchy and grumpy.

They spend half their lives complaining, living in the land of sadness and sullenness. They give to those around them, each day, the "gift" of complaining. The irony is that they might not have been born to live a life of complaining and lamenting.

Be grateful and thankful you are alive. Have fun. Live in the grace of God.

Yes, there is much in the world to be sad about. There is much to complain about. There is much misery and suffering. And we do not need to be persons who add to the sadness, misery, and suffering. We are not the people of the wet blanket. We are not the people of the cross, finally.

We are the people of Easter. We are the people of wonder and joy. We are the people of the great banquet. We are the people of the wedding feast. We rejoice. We have fun. We live with happiness. We live in the grace of God.

God surrounds us with people who know how to have fun, who, even amidst the dark depressions, sad events of life, deep tragedies that befall them, know the joy of life, having a capacity for fun, to laugh and carry on, having a good time. It is an art worth our learning. There are times of sadness. In the grace of God, there are many times of fun and gladness, wonder, and joy.

God wants us to know the joy of life, to share in the laughter of good fun and good times. God gives us people who have discovered how to share joy and laughter so that we might discover this precious gift, that our lives might be whole and healthy.

The capacity to learn how to relax and have fun is an extraordinary gift you can give to yourself. Indeed, as we relax and have fun, we give this gift to all of those around us. Laughter is contagious. Relaxing relaxes those around us. When we have fun, those around us have fun.

We are too often tense and tight, nervous and anxious, mostly over things that, in the long haul of life, amount to very little. We allow ourselves to be distracted by petty matters that are of minor consequence. We become preoccupied with these small difficulties, and in the process we become tense and tight, unable to relax.

We help ourselves relax when we have a few objectives that are specific and concrete, realistic and achievable, with solid time horizons. If we create too many goals, set them too high, expect them to be accomplished too soon, then we become overwhelmed, unable to relax and have fun. As we keep our eye on a few objectives, looking to God, we can more easily relax.

If we do not know the few goals that count, then everything becomes an important and urgent goal, to be accomplished immediately, now or even sooner. We end up with too many goals, with too little time, and we take our eyes off the few objectives that, in fact, count. We become distracted, busily seeking to do too much, too soon. We are tense and tight.

Mostly, we worry over matters that are minor and inconsequential. Or, we worry about matters over which we have no control. When you worry, worry over a worry worth worrying about. Worry about something worthwhile. Worry over something you can do something about.

Then, having worried in a worthwhile way, relax. When you go to bed at night and cannot quite go to sleep for worrying over something, ask yourself, "Is this a worry worth worrying about?" Then ask yourself, "Is this a worry I can do something about?" Then, relax and go to sleep.

The worries that are worth worrying about and that you can do something about can be tackled when you are in the freshest, best position to do something about them—in the morning. The other, lesser worries, give over to God. God will worry about those for you. Let them go. Learn to whisper, "Oh, God . . ." and let it be a whispered prayer. When you feel you have more piled on you than you can do, you help yourself get it all into perspective by whispering, "Oh, God . . ." Let God fill in the blank.

This reminds you that you are not alone, and that you are never asked to do more than you and God together can handle. Call on your silent partner—this God with the amazing sense of grace and humor—to help you get beyond the current overwhelming situations so you can both enjoy the fun of it together.

Be at peace. Relax. Discover new ways you can have fun. For each worry worth really worrying about, that you can do something about, discover one new way you can have fun in this life. For each significant worry, find some significant way of having fun. Your life will have a sense of balance, health, and wholeness.

God laughs. The omnipotent, omniscient, all-powerful, all-knowing, saving being-above-all-beings, the holy, Lord God almighty, maker and ruler of all things, laughs. Yes, God knows of our times of suffering. We have experienced times of suffering and pain, knowing that God is with us. We know also that God gives us new life. God's spirit is of joy and wonder. God is Christmas. God is Easter. God is Pentecost.

Jesus laughs. I have a copy of a picture of Jesus laughing. The laughter—you can see and feel it in the picture—is good-natured and gentle, understanding and joyful. Think of it. With all around him and all before him, Jesus laughs. He describes wedding feasts and great banquets. He shares wonder and joy, new life and hope.

A phrase came to me late one night, gently and invitingly, quietly and peacefully: "Relax, have fun, enjoy life, live in the grace of God." I have shared that phrase in seminars around the planet.

People share with me that they have put the phrase on their mirror, so they see it first thing in the morning. Pastors teach me that the phrase sits on their pulpit, and each Sunday, when they begin the service, they begin with this spirit. People put the phrase on the screen saver of their computer. Countless persons share that this is their prayer as they go to bed at night.

People describe how, in the midst of joyful events, the phrase comes to them. Many persons share how, in the midst of difficult times, these words see them through. As we learn how to relax and have fun, in the deepest sense possible, we are more able to live lives of joy, deeply and profoundly. For a whole, healthy life, it is helpful that you have fun in life. Look forward to having fun in your life.

Where persons have fun, there is the grace of God.

Prayer

Living and loving God, help us to have fun. In the midst of the sad worries and difficult dilemmas of life, help us to discover the wonder and joy of living. Grant us days of sunshine and blue skies, of grace and peace. When life is filled with darkness and doubt, give us wedding feasts of grace and great banquets of hope. Fill our days with Christmas and Easter. May we live with happiness and joyfulness.

With the grace of God, we pray.

Amen.

4. VALUE EXCELLENT MISTAKES

The Coral Reef

We value excellent mistakes.
We live in the grace of God.

A decisive event in my own life is a sail to the Bahamas. A decisive discovery in my own life is my learning of excellent mistakes.

On our first trip to the Bahamas, we left Florida early in the evening, sailing a remarkable thirty-five-foot boat. It would sleep six persons and included a full galley, shower, and head. The mainsail and genoa provided an extraordinary spread of sail. Our destination was Bimini, the nearest landfall to Florida across the Gulf Stream. We had learned from various people who had made the crossing that the best way was to sail all night long, arriving early in the morning at Bimini.

The entrance to the harbor is long and narrow. It turns frequently. There are coral reefs and sandbars, creating a twisting, winding course. The challenge is to weave your way among the reefs and sandbars to the harbor. If you leave Florida in the morning, you get there at nighttime and have to anchor offshore until the next morning. By arriving early in the morning, a person standing on the bow can see the reefs. The water is so clear, you can see almost forever. With these sightings from the bow, you can navigate between the reefs.

I can still see my parents standing on the dock in Ft. Lauderdale and waving goodbye to their two grandsons, as Julie and I and our two sons left Florida. My parents were convinced, given that we were sailing through what is known as the Bermuda Triangle, that this could be the last time they might see their grandsons alive.

During the crossing that night, we had some of the best sailing I've known in my whole life. I remember around two or two-thirty in the morning, everybody was asleep below. The seas were gentle and rolling. The wind was strong, but not too much. We were making good time. I was at the tiller sailing toward a cluster of stars—not one star, a cluster. It was some of the most incredible sailing I have ever known.

Early that morning, we sighted Bimini. We had stayed the course well. We saw a freighter just off Bimini near the channel. Freighters need deep water. We concluded that if we stayed near the freighter, we would be in deep water and would miss the coral reefs. We stayed steady, moving closer, yet closer, and yet closer to the freighter.

There was a grinding crunch.

One never quite forgets the crunch of the keel of a sailboat on a coral reef. We ran aground near the center of the reef. We soon found out that three days before, the captain of the freighter, who had been sailing twenty-plus years in the Bahamas, had run his freighter onto the center of the coral reef. There it remained.

The closer we got to the freighter, the closer we got to the coral reef.

Our sailboat was now listing dangerously to starboard, then abruptly to port. Back and forth. Back and forth. With the help of a native fisherman and his fishing boat, we got our sailboat off the reef with no damage done—remarkable in that respect. We found our way safely into the Bimini harbor, made our way to a berth and began to calm down after the tension of hitting a coral reef.

We learned that there is a saying in the Bahamas, where there are lots of reefs and shallow water: "If a skipper says he has never run aground, his boat has never left the dock."

VALUE EXCELLENT MISTAKES

Value excellent mistakes. You will live in the grace of God.

One key, one possibility, for a whole, healthy life is creativity. God invites us to a life of creativity, not a routine, habituated life, dull and sluggish, tediously the same. Creativity is a wonderful resource, and you can nurture it by developing your capacity to learn from your mistakes, your capacity to learn from your achievements, your spirit of flexibility, and your capacity to learn in a rich variety of ways.

One resource for creativity is the capacity to learn from our mistakes. We make mistakes. Likely, we make more mistakes than we ever imagined or wanted to. Some are minor, incidental ones. Some mistakes are major, grievous ones. It is one thing to confess our mistakes. It is another thing to learn from them. Confession is most helpful. Learning from our mistakes is most helpful. There is little point in continuing to repeat the same mistakes.

We can learn from the minor, incidental mistakes that are part of daily living. We try something simple. It does not work. We try something else. That doesn't work. Finally, we discover some way forward that works. With minor, incidental activities, we are able to nurture our capacity to learn from our mistakes.

Some mistakes are major, grievous mistakes. They are harmful to the ones we love, to the people around us, and frequently to ourselves. They are the troubling, damaging mistakes, disturbing and injurious. The memory of them is sometimes more than we can bear. We are overcome with the damage these mistakes have done. We wish they had never happened.

These mistakes I refer to as *excellent mistakes*. They are really good mistakes. Now, I do not mean to discount the serious damage that these mistakes cause. Rather, I use the term *excellent mistakes* to confirm that they are among the best mistakes we have made. They are major mistakes. They do much damage and harm.

The more positive the recognition for excellent mistakes, the higher the level of creativity in one's life. Positive recognition means that we acknowledge the mistake and we learn from our mistake. Positive recognition does not mean praising or condoning the mistake that is made. Rather, it means owning up to the mistake, asking for forgiveness, and especially learning from the mistake. It is one thing to confess our mistakes. It is another thing to learn from them. It is an excellent mistake when we learn well from it.

The more negative the recognition of excellent mistakes, the lower the level of creativity in one's life. Negative recognition of mistakes causes people to try never to make a mistake. Further, negative recognition causes them, when they do make a serious mistake, to seek to repress the mistake. They, thereby, become frozen in the mistake and do not learn from it.

The art is to learn from our mistakes, rather than become frozen by them. When we allow ourselves to make a mistake, we allow ourselves to be creative. It is not that we purposely try to make mistakes, but when we do not allow ourselves to make a mistake, we do not allow ourselves to be creative. The art is to sail forward, not to freeze at the dock. Ships are meant for sailing, not staying at the dock. We are meant for living, not being frozen, fearful and frightened, never leaving the dock.

The creative inventors of our time, and of all previous times, developed the capacity to learn from their mistakes. Indeed, it is only after countless experiments—what I call excellent mistakes—that they come to their discoveries. You will note that I said they *developed the capacity to learn from their mistakes.* The capacity to learn from one's mistakes is a learned behavior pattern.Regrettably, some people learn they should never make a mistake.

Regrettably, well-intentioned persons taught them this behavior pattern. Whatever they do, they must never *be* a mistake. When people are told frequently enough to never make a mistake, they sometimes conclude, if they ever make one, that they are the mistake. Making a mistake and being a mistake become one and the same. To make a mistake is to be a mistake.

Well-meaning persons whose message to others is to "never make a mistake" think they are teaching a behavior pattern of excellence. But, the lesson people learn is to never make a mistake. The best way to never make a mistake is to never try anything.

For some people, staying at the dock, never setting sail, is, for them, the way to never make a mistake. These people are not lazy, indolent, and sluggish. They have a deeper, more serious dilemma. Their compulsive, addictive perfectionism causes them to never do anything so they will never fail.

Creativity is lost.

The beginning of creativity is developing the capacity to learn from one's mistakes. As we remember the mistakes of the past and present, it does not help to denigrate oneself, to punish oneself, to look down on oneself, or to develop doubt about oneself. The art is to value what we learn from our mistakes. When we learn and grow from our mistakes, we encourage our best creativity.

When we deliver positive recognition for excellent mistakes, when we help people learn and grow from their excellent mistakes, we encourage their best spirit of creativity. When we deliver negative recognition for mistakes, when we press people to never make a mistake, we teach them that the best way to never make a mistake is for their boat to never leave the dock.

Ships are meant for sailing, not for docking. For a whole, healthy life, it is helpful for you to value excellent mistakes.

Where persons value excellent mistakes, there is the grace of God.

43

Prayer

Gracious and Forgiving God, we are thankful for your generous forgiveness of our excellent mistakes, our grievous sins, and our foolish errors. We remember them with pain and remorse. Our sorrow is more than we can bear. We are grateful for your spirit of forgiveness. Help us to forgive ourselves. Help us to be as generous with ourselves as you are with us. Help us to value and learn from our mistakes.

With the grace of God, we pray.

Amen.

5. BUILD ON YOUR STRENGTHS

Harold and Steve

We build on our strengths.
We live in the grace of God.

Two decisive events in my own life are two baseball teams and two seasons. The decisive persons are Harold and Steve, from whom I have learned much.

On one team, during one season, one of my players, Harold, all season long, kept jumping up and down, "Coach, let me pitch, let me pitch, let me pitch." After a while you get tired of the pleading and whining. In one game, toward the end of the season, I started him as pitcher.

We were still in the first inning. The other team was having a field day at bat. They had the bases loaded. There were no outs. We were now nine runs behind. And, it was still the first inning.

One of the hardest things I have ever had to do was walk out to the pitcher's mound, in what I hoped would be near the end of the first inning. I said to Harold, "This is my fault. This is my mistake. I should have been out here five runs ago. You are our best short-stop. Please, now, go play shortstop. Sam is coming in as pitcher. With your fielding, the rest of the team's fielding, and Sam's pitching, we will get out of this inning and beyond this game." We did.

Harold played the best shortstop he had played all season.

Another season. Another team. An important game. I started Steve as pitcher. We were in the first inning. The other team had men on all three bases. There were no outs. We were now four runs behind.

I said to myself, "I've been here before." I called a time out. I walked out to the mound. Steve was glad to see me coming. He was not eager to continue. As I drew near, Steve started to step off the mound. He handed me the ball.

I handed the ball back to him. I said, "Steve, I don't know what in the name of heaven you think you are doing out here, but you had better figure it out pretty quick, because you are the only one who is going to pitch this whole game."

He did. He pitched himself out of the inning. He pitched the whole game. With confidence and assurance, he found his stride and rhythm. We won the game by one run.

Harold's gifts are at shortstop. Steve's gifts are at pitcher. God blesses both.

BUILD ON YOUR STRENGTHS

Build on your strengths. You will live in the grace of God.

We look for, we build on the strengths we really have, not the ones we wish we had. When we look for the strengths we wish we had, we miss the strengths we really have. In tough, tight times, stick with, build on, your strengths.

The art is to build on the strengths you have, not the ones you wish you had. Harold had spent too much time preoccupied with the gift he wished he had, and not enough time on the gift he really had, namely, playing shortstop. Steve was about to give up on his real gift, pitching. With encouragement, he came into his own. He became our best pitcher.

The art of building on your strengths is a matter of life. It is matter of theology. We do not build on our strengths so we can think better of ourselves. It is not finally a matter of self-worth, self-esteem, or positive thinking. It is not finally rooted in us. We are claiming the grace of God in our lives. We live a theology of grace. We claim our strengths as a matter of grace.

Ephesians 2:8

For by grace, are ye saved through faith;
and that not of yourselves;
it is the gift of God.

I understand the text to include this spirit:

For by grace, we are given these strengths;
and these are not of our own doing;
they are the gifts of God.

When you build on your strengths, you build on God's gifts. Whatever strengths, gifts, and competencies you build on, you build on them as gifts of God's grace. When you build on your strengths, you live with confidence and assurance, with an encouraging spirit in the gifts with which God has blessed and is blessing you. When you build on your strengths, you live in the grace of God.

Sometimes, we claim our strengths. Then, we become preoccupied with our weaknesses. Mistakenly, we assume that once we claim our strengths we should then focus on our weaknesses and shortcomings. The art, once we claim our strengths, gifts, and competencies, is to build on our current strengths. We do better what we do best.

Harold plays a better shortstop. He builds on his gift of fielding grounders. Steve builds on his gift of pitching fastballs. You and I take one of our current strengths and grow forward our competency and ability in this current strength. We build forward the gift with which God is blessing us.

Of a given morning, when you first arise, build on your strengths. It is not that you build on your strengths once, in a given year, and then move on in living your life. That old friend "worry" will show up— worry that you are not doing enough about a weakness. Then, that old friend "a compulsive, addictive compulsiveness" will try to get back into your life. You will allow yourself to be distracted, lured into focusing on a weakness. Low self-esteem will give you unpleasant company.

For a whole, healthy life, it is helpful that you confirm the strengths on which you are building. As you build on your strengths—and you will—you will discover grace and peace are good friends in your life. They will walk with you. Each day, as you build on your strengths, you build the richness of your life. Build on your strengths. Live in the grace of God.

Where persons build on their strengths, there is the grace of God.

Prayer

Gracious and Loving God, we are thankful for your generous gifts of strengths and competencies in our lives. We are amazed at your generosity. We are grateful for your spirit of encouragement—for your blessings in our lives. Help us to build on our strengths. Help us to not be preoccupied with our weaknesses. Help us to grow forward what we do best—with joy and wonder, gratitude and grace.

With the grace of God, we pray.

Amen.

6. LIVE PROGRESS

Sweet Silence and Hilda Mae

We live progress.
We live in the grace of God.

A decisive discovery in my own life is my learning of a life of progress, not perfection. Two decisive persons in my life are Sweet Silence and Hilda Mae.

I met Sweet Silence and Hilda Mae during a seminar I was leading for about five hundred people. Sweet Silence and her sister, Hilda Mae, had asked to visit with me over lunch one day during the three-day event. We had a remarkable lunch. We laughed and carried on. We shared stories with one another. We have shared with one another over the years that have come and gone.

Both sisters are short of stature, with gentle eyes, calm faces, and quiet, easy dispositions. They live together, helping one another in their early retirement years. Neither has ever married. Hilda Mae came close twice, but for whatever reason, each proposed wedding never happened. I asked them to share with me something about their lives, where they were born, and what had happened since. Each of them shared her life's story.

Sweet Silence lives a life of progress, not perfectionism. She began being called by that name early in her life because of her plain, sweet personality and because of her quiet, unassuming ways. When I think of Sweet Silence, I think of Francis of Assisi's statement, "Go and preach the Gospel. Use words if necessary." For Sweet Silence, words are hardly ever necessary.

In a natural, spontaneous, generous way, she shares the richness of her life and her help with people around her. Sharing just enough help to be helpful—but not so much help that it becomes harmful—she is a wonderful Good Samaritan with her family and friends, and, indeed, with the whole community.

She is a legend for her hopeful, encouraging spirit and her generous kindness. Her spirit is one of progress, not perfectionism. Gently, graciously, she lives one day at a time. She has solid self-esteem. She is grateful God loves her and thinks well of her.

She has a gift for encouraging people, not a drive for controlling and directing. Her life is lived with generous kindness and a gentle, gracious spirit. She is preoccupied neither with wishful thinking nor with an excessive drive toward achievement. She thinks in terms of a few key objectives that are helpful, realistic, achievable, and have solid time horizons. She has a confident sense of hope.

By contrast, Hilda Mae, her sister, lives a life of compulsive addictive perfectionism. In her own quiet, persistent manner, learned from somewhere or someone, she shares a spirit of compulsive addictive perfectionism. Somehow, she developed low self-esteem; she thinks more poorly of herself than she has a right to think. A compulsive addictive perfectionism and low self-esteem go together. Compulsive perfectionism yields low self-esteem. Low self-esteem yields an overcompensating, compulsive perfectionism.

These two dynamics together helped her develop a tendency toward controlling and directing, mostly other people. She seems always to be about carefully devising what people should do. In her overcompensating manner, she develops an excessive drive toward achievement. Her tendency is to set too many goals, too high, to be accomplished too soon, mostly for other people.

Then, she develops a kind of worried, wishful thinking that someone will come and save the day. A few times, this has happened. Someone or some group has come and saved the day for her. Regrettably, this has simply reinforced the intertwining dynamics of perfectionism: low self-esteem; a tendency toward controlling and directing; an excessive drive toward achievement; and a worried, wishful thinking that someone will come and save the day.

Hilda Mae does good works, carefully planned and carried out virtually to perfection. Nothing is ever out of place. Everything is in order. She has a tidy spirit about life. Hilda Mae almost never gets upset. She is not mean-spirited. She never raises her voice. People have never seen her angry or distressed. She seldom weeps. Her spirit feels cautious and constricted.

Quiet and determined, she goes about her life and work. People do sense she always attaches some strings to her helping. It is as if she says (without speaking), "I will help you with this. And then I want you to do that." She seeks to control with kindness. She gives gifts with strings.

For Sweet Silence, Life Is	For Hilda Mae, Life Is
Progress	Compulsive perfectionism
Solid self-esteem	Low self-esteem
Encouraging spirit	Tendency to controlling, directing
Generous kindness	Careful devising
Gentle, gracious spirit	Excessive drive to achieve
Few key objectives, well done	Too many goals, set too high, too soon
Confident sense of hope	Worried, wishful thinking

Natural, spontaneous grace   Cautious, constricted law
Spirit of trust   Spirit of doubt

Grace and life, creativity and objectives, strengths and mission—we share them with a spirit of progress, not a compulsion toward perfectionism. A healthy life and a healthy mission—with abundant creativity and solid objectives—have about them a gentle, moving spirit of progress, not a compulsive addictive perfectionism.

Progress does not mean that things are always getting better and better, always moving upward and higher. Progress is a matter of living life one day at a time, one step at a time. Progress is learning the art of relaxing, having fun, enjoying life, and living in the grace of God.

Both a spirit of progress and a compulsion toward perfectionism are learned patterns of behavior. The harder of the two to learn is a compulsion toward perfectionism. Compulsive perfectionism goes against the grain of whom and whose God creates us to be. Perfectionism requires more energy, drive, and determination because we are working against whom God intends us to be. It is easier to learn a spirit of progress. If we can learn the harder one, perfectionism, we can learn the easier one, progress.

Sweet Silence and Hilda Mae are both wonderful women. Again and again, people have taught me that it is easier to have a relationship with Sweet Silence than it is with Hilda Mae. Sweet Silence accepts people for who they are. Hilda Mae, with her compulsion toward perfectionism, is always trying to get people to be slightly better than who they now are. There is a strain in Hilda Mae's relationships.

Sweet Silence has, with people, a natural, spontaneous, generous basis of the relationships. There is no strain. The relationships with Sweet Silence are relaxed and easy going.

It is interesting how Sweet Silence, with a spirit of spontaneous generosity, is helpful with those people around her. Her acts of serving and helping come naturally. There doesn't seem to be much of a plan about them. By contrast, Hilda Mae carefully devises and plans, then delays, delays, and delays. She delays because she wants to be sure she gets it precisely right.

When people are around Sweet Silence, they discover their own best creativity. When people are around Hilda Mae, they always have the feeling that her acts of kindness are a way of controlling and directing them toward those ends that she has in mind for them, that she knows are best for them.

LIVE PROGRESS

Live progress. You will live in the grace of God.

Progress, not perfectionism. This is a key, key learning for life. When we live a life of progress, we live a life in the grace of God. When we live life with a compulsive addictive perfectionism, we are never, finally, satisfied with ourselves or with those around us. We tend to deny our strengths. Our compassion becomes compulsion. We become preoccupied with our weaknesses, and with other people's shortcomings. We are always striving for "more."

The tragedy is that a compulsive addictive perfectionism works. Many of us have achieved what we have attained because of an onboard, active, compulsive, persistent perfectionism. It worked. The trouble—the difficulty—is that we have had to spend massive amounts of emotional energy, time, and effort to make that way of living work. We have had to swim against the current of who God intends us to be. We have strained our relationships with our loved ones and our friends.

When we discover a life of progress, we achieve richer, fuller results with a more relaxed spirit of grace and peace. We are less hard on ourselves, our loved ones, and our friends. Life is deeper, more fun, and more fulfilling. We discover the gift of happiness.

We share comfort and joy. We are at our most relaxed best. We live in the grace of God.

Some persons, some families, some groupings are like Sweet Silence. They encourage grace and life, creativity and objectives. They are strong and healthy, flourishing, and having fun. They live a life of progress. They have solid self-esteem and an encouraging spirit. They value generous kindness and a gentle, gracious spirit. They set a few key objectives. They have a confident sense of hope. They live with a natural, spontaneous grace and a spirit of trust.

Some persons, some families, some groupings are like Hilda Mae. Regrettably, they learned a compulsive addictive perfectionism. They suffer from low self-esteem. They have a tendency to controlling and directing more than an interest in creativity and objectives. They control with careful kindness. They develop, with polite courtesy and benevolent thoughtfulness, a cautious devising of what the people around them should do.

Sometimes, we learn a compulsive addictive perfectionism from a loved one who "sought the best for us." They intended well. Most likely, they learned a compulsive addictive perfectionism from some loved one who intended well for them.

Sometimes, we learn a compulsive addictive perfectionism as our way of overcompensating for low self-esteem. The two are, regrettably, good friends. A compulsive addictive perfectionism sets up too many goals, set too high, to be accomplished too soon. We sense we have set ourselves up to fail.

We postpone action to postpone failure. The cause is not procrastination. That is the symptom. The real cause is an active compulsive addictive perfectionism.

Progress has an encouraging spirit. Healthy, effective persons, families, and groupings begin to emerge. We build on our strengths with a relaxed intentionality. We are not rushed. We are not hurried. We set reasonable objectives, a few, realistic and achievable, with solid time horizons. Grace and life, mission and service move forward. The future begins to look promising for many people.

I have the honor of knowing many persons, families, and groupings who have a spirit of progress, a sense of solid self-esteem, and an encouraging spirit with persons. They are gifted with generous kindness, a gentle and gracious spirit, and a few key objectives well done. They share a confident sense of hope. They have a natural and spontaneous grace. They share a spirit of trust in the grace of God and in one another. The signs of a healthy life, the gifts of creativity are in the life of Sweet Silence.

Of a given morning, when you first arise, live, *this day,* with a spirit of progress. It is not that you decide on a life of progress once, and then you move on in living your life, falling, likely, back into perfectionism. Things will come up. You will get busy. People with an onboard perfectionism will try to influence you. You will begin to revert. You will develop forgetfulness. You will slide back. A compulsion toward perfectionism will try, sneakily and silently, to creep back in.

Of a given morning, decide to live a day like Sweet Silence. Decide to not live a day like Hilda Mae. I encourage you to confirm a life of progress. As you live life with this spirit of progress, your compassion will deepen, your strengths will grow, and you will build a whole, healthy life. You will live life with grace and peace.

Where persons live progress, there is the grace of God.

Prayer

Almighty and Everlasting God, who art ever faithful
with us, we pray you will fill us with grace and peace.
Help us to be at peace with our lives. Grant us days
of comfort and contentment. Help us to not be restless
with perfectionism. Give us days of progress. May we
be ever in your arms of mercy and kindness. May
we be as kind with ourselves as you are with us.

With the grace of God, we pray.

Amen.

7. LET GO

The Slipping Anchor

We let go.
We live in the grace of God.

A decisive event in my own life is a slipping anchor. The decisive persons are Julie, and our sons, Ken and Mike.

We were sailing that year in the Bahamas, Julie and I and Mike and Ken, our five- and seven-year-old sons. We had a wonderful sailboat we had chartered. We were having a grand time.

Late one afternoon, a storm came up. The seas began to roll and rise. We learned over the shortwave that, far off, a hurricane was swirling. We were getting the fringe effect from the hurricane. The seas became uncomfortably high, choppy, and rough. We headed toward a deserted island—a *key*, they call them in the Bahamas. According to the map, there was a small harbor where we could anchor our boat and be protected from the storm.

Near dusk, we made our way into the little harbor of the deserted island. The island was smaller than the map made it appear, and there was a huge coral reef toward the back and on one side of the harbor. We set our anchor to ride out the storm that night. The little bit of beach and island did block the waves from us. It was comparatively comfortable. We settled in.

It wasn't too long before the boat began to drift toward the coral reef. The anchor had slipped. We pulled the anchor up, repositioned the boat with the inboard motor, dropped the anchor on what we thought would be firmer bottom, and began to make preparations for the night. Not too much later, the anchor slipped again. We set it again.

As we went to bed that night, we decided to stand watch so that, should the anchor slip yet another time, we would not find ourselves on the coral reef. So here were a five-year-old and a seven-year-old, Julie, and I taking turns at watch that night. The anchor did slip several times. I would be awakened, if it was not my watch. We would set the anchor and it would last for a while. Then, we would have to set it again.

In the morning, after a nearly sleepless night, we could see that the storm out in the ocean was continuing in its fury. The storm was not going anywhere, nor were we.

The harbor clearly had a soft bottom and anchors would not hold, so I decided to do what is sometimes done, namely carry the anchor to shore, carry it up the beach a ways, bury it deep into the beach, and then it would hold.

Julie had the inboard motor going slowly, just moving us forward toward the beach. I was standing on the bow of the boat, holding this humongous anchor in my arms, looking down into the water. It was clear. The water in the Bahamas is so clear you can see almost forever.

I stepped off into what I thought was shallow water. Halfway down, it dawned on me that if I let go of the anchor I would quit sinking. The anchor was fixed to the boat by a chain and a line. I was the one in trouble, sinking rapidly. I let go. I quit sinking.

That event has occasioned a saying in our family, to be, I am sure, passed down from one generation to the next: "If you want to sink fast, be sure to hold on to an anchor."

LET GO

Let go. You will live in the grace of God.

Now, I know, in one sense, God is our anchor. I also know we all carry around with us quiet grudges, deep resentments, hushed bitterness, low-grade hostility, subliminal anger, and occasional eruptive forms of rage. All these weigh us down. As long as we carry them around with us, we continue sinking in this life. Let them go.

Ships are meant for sailing, not for being at anchor. We are meant for sailing, not for allowing ourselves to be pulled down by the anchors we carry around with us.

We can paraphrase the text in Hebrews:

Hebrews 12:1

*"Wherefore, seeing we also are compassed about
with so great a cloud of witnesses,*

*let us lay aside every weight, grudge, anger,
bitterness, resentment, encumbrance, impediment,
and the sin that so weighs us down,
and let us run steadily the course set before us. . . ."*

God invites us to lay aside our resentments, grudges, and bitterness. They only weigh us down. They cause us to sink. With God's help, we lay them aside, we let them go, and run well the race God gives us.

Of a morning, when you first arise, live, *this day,* with a spirit of "let go." Select one resentment, one bitterness, one anger, or one guilt you plan to give up for today. It is not that you decide on a life of "let go" once, and then you move on in living your life, carrying around your resentments and bitternesses, weighing you down.

Anxiety will show up. Resentment will rear its ugly head. Grudge will join the conversation. You will begin to relapse.

LET GO. LET GOD.

Of a morning, decide one weight to let go of. For a whole, healthy life, it is helpful that you confirm a life of "let go." As you live life with this spirit of "let go," your compassion will deepen, your strengths will grow, and you will experience more fun and happiness in your life. You will live life with grace and peace.

Where persons let go, there is the grace of God.

Prayer

Living and Generous God, we pray you will help us to let go of resentments and bitterness, guilt and grudge. We weigh ourselves down. Life is too heavy for us. We pray you will lighten our load. Help us to live with grace and peace, to love one another, and to love ourselves, even as you love us.

With the grace of God, we pray.

Amen.

8. COMPASSION RUNS

The Running Father

We run with compassion.
We live in the grace of God.

A decisive event in my own life is my discovery of the grace of this text. I was in my study. The early morning sun was coming up. The day would be warm and beautiful. The sunlight was breaking on the top of Mt. Princeton, with its pale pink glow.

We would have pancakes and syrup, eggs and bacon for breakfast. I would continue my study of Luke. Later in the day, Julie and I would journey to St. Elmo, an ancient mining town near the top of Mt. Princeton, to feed the chipmunks and to have a picnic.

For now, I was giving myself to a study of the Gospel of Luke. In Luke 15:20, we read:

"But when he was yet a great way off, his father saw him, and had compassion, and ran, and fell on his neck, and kissed him . . . ."

The text came alive for me. The key to the text is what the father does.

Yes, the prodigal son does come home. It is important we discover this.

The real key to the text is what the father does.

The father runs.

The key words in the text are *compassion* and *ran*. Sometimes, I call this text "The Parable of the Loving Father." Yet, *loving* does not fully describe what the father does. The father is the loving, *running* father. The father *runs* with compassion. Thus, more often, I call this "The Parable of the Running Father."

Luke 15:20–24

And he arose, and came to his father.
But when he was yet a great way off,
his father saw him, and had compassion,
and ran, and fell on his neck and kissed him.

And the son said unto him, Father, I have sinned
against heaven, and in thy sight, and
am no more worthy to be called thy son.

But the father said to his servants,
Bring forth the best robe, and put it on him;
and put a ring on his hand,
and shoes on his feet:

And bring hither the fatted calf, and kill it;
and let us eat, and be merry:

For this my son was dead, and is alive again;
he was lost, and is found.
And they began to be merry.

Compassion runs. Forgiveness runs, generously, fully. Reconciliation runs. Compassion is the spirit of the soul. Grow your compassion, generously and fully. Compassion does not walk. Compassion runs.

The good news of the text is: "*But when he was yet a great way off, his father saw him, and had compassion, and ran, and fell on his neck, and kissed him . . . .*" The father said to his servants, 'Bring forth the best robe, and put it on him; and put a ring on his hand, and shoes on his feet; and bring hither the fatted calf and kill it, and let us eat and make merry; for this my son was dead, and is alive again; he was lost, and is found' " (Luke 15:20, 22–24).

The servants bring the robe of compassion, the ring of community, and the sandals of hope. The feast is gathered. They eat and make merry. They rejoice. There is much happiness, joy, and laughter. All of this happens because the father runs to his son.

COMPASSION RUNS

Run with compassion. You will live in the grace of God.

The far country to which we sometimes carry ourselves is the kingdom of deep resentments, quiet grudges, and hushed bitternesses. It is not a pleasant place. It is a pigsty, muck and mud, where we wallow in our own fears and angers, resentments and rages. We waste the inheritance God gives us.

What you can count on and depend upon is this: God runs to you with compassion. While you are yet a long way off, God runs to you. God does not wait. God does not walk. God runs. God welcomes you home. God throws loving arms around you, and calls for the robe and the ring, the sandals, and to kill the fatted calf; because you who were dead are now alive. You who were lost are now found.

The text is grace, not law.

Regrettably, sometimes you and I write the gospel text in a rules-and-regulations, conditions-and-stipulations, policies-and-procedures, legalistic way. Even with loved ones, friends, family, we sometimes write the text this way:

While the young son was yet a long way off, the father saw him, and he remembered their last bitter parting. He remembered hearing that the inheritance had been squandered in a far country.

So he waited in the house until the young son drew nigh. He did not move. The young son knocked once. The father waited. A second time the young son knocked. The father did not move. He waited in the house. A third time the young son knocked. Finally, the father rose and went slowly to the door.

He opened the door, and his son fell on his knees and said, "Father, I have sinned against heaven and before thee. I am no longer worthy to be called thy son. Take me back as one of thy hired servants."

There was a long, long, long silence.

Finally, the father said, "Well, who is this? Do I know you? Come in. We will have a long, long talk, one like we used to have. If I am to take you back, there will be ninety-seven conditions and stipulations, policies and procedures, rules and regulations; and if, after five years of dutiful and faithful commitment, you break yea not a single one, I may then yet call you my son."

Good friends, we sometimes do this, yea, even with loved ones, family, and friends. We allow our bitterness and grudges, our resentment and anger to get the best of us. We wait in the house, with lecture, admonition, and scolding at hand.

What the gospel text says, what the good news is, is that while the young son was yet a long way off, his father saw him, and had compassion, and ran to him and welcomed him home. "He had compassion." These are three of the most helpful, hopeful words we will ever hear.

God runs to you with compassion. God invites you to run with compassion. God welcomes you home with compassion. God invites you to welcome home friends, loved ones, strangers with compassion. The time to wait is over. The time to run has come. Run well, with compassion.

Where persons run with compassion, there is the grace of God.

Prayer

Almighty and Everloving God, we are grateful you run to us with your compassion, even as we are yet a long way off. Forgive our wanderings in a far country. We are amazed that you welcome us home, with a cloak of compassion, a ring of community, and sandals of hope. We are overwhelmed with your grace.

With the grace of God, we pray.

Amen.

9. HUMILITY AND WISDOM

Dr. Politella

We live humility and wisdom.
We live in the grace of God.

A decisive event in my own life is my student days in the study of philosophy. The decisive person is Dr. Politella.

Dr. Politella was a gifted teacher. I can see him now. Thin body, small of stature, slightly bent forward at the shoulders, hands clasped in front, he relished each new idea as a radiant discovery and taught us the wisdom of the ages. His voice was soft and mellow, almost hushed. It was as though he were bowing with humility before the truth, reverently, quietly sharing.

The class leaned forward to catch each precious, thoughtful word, to hear the wisdom his almost whispery voice shared. His gentle, warm smile, his enthusiasm for discernment, for insight, for meaning in life drew the class to new discoveries.

He had a gentle manner. His dark hair was combed back, lying flat. His glasses were perched forward on his nose, almost ready to fall off. He always wore a dark suit, with a subtle tie neatly in place. His tender smile was like the gentle dawning of a new day, the miracle of wisdom in his face. That is how I remember Dr. Politella.

Dr. Politella was my central, inspiring, amazing teacher at the university.

Some years later, I learned from my parents that my high school guidance counselor had taken them aside and advised them that there was no point in my going to college. I had been active in this club and that club, president of this organization and that organization, master counselor of the DeMolay chapter, on the varsity debate team, and I had made mostly Cs in my grades.

He told them that Cs become Ds in college, and, therefore, there was no point in my going. It would be a waste of money. I was better suited to some trade. Fortunately, they did not share that "counsel" with me for some years to come.

Yes, when I went to the university, I had to learn things I should have learned in high school so I could understand what I was supposed to be learning at the university. Fortunately, I had many excellent professors in my first year. Because of my excellent grades the first quarter, I was awarded an academic scholarship, and I continued to be awarded the scholarship throughout my academic years of study.

I took a philosophy course with Dr. Politella during my first quarter. From then on, across my four years at the university, I had the honor of taking all of the courses he taught. He became my professor for my philosophy major, and the most revered respected professor in the university.

His teaching was extraordinary. He radiated wisdom. His way of teaching was sacramental in spirit, an outward, visible sign of the inner, spiritual gift of wisdom. The joy of discovery, the wonder of a new idea, the gift of a new insight, he was all of these.

He loved to share the history of ideas: Plato, Aristotle, and the philosophers of the ages, come and gone. Eastern philosophy, historical philosophy, contemporary philosophy, mysticism, logic, ethics—the range of subjects in which he was deeply conversant was remarkable.

Mostly, he shared wisdom. He helped us think and encouraged us to discover wisdom, think deeply and fully, see in the obvious the deeper meanings of life, look beyond the apparent. He taught us humility and meekness before the truth. He taught us wisdom and judgment, compassion and common sense.

Dr. Politella joined the philosophy faculty of Kent State University in 1947. I had the honor of studying with him from 1954 to 1958. From 1958 to 1962, I had the honor of studying with a wondrous faculty at Perkins School of Theology at Southern Methodist University for my M.Div. degree. Then, again I continued my studies at Perkins from 1965 to 1967 for my S.T.M. degree. In 1974, I earned my Ph.D. from Emory University, with a remarkable faculty there.

In the intervening years, I have had the privilege of knowing, working with, and sharing with many persons who have known something of wisdom. Some have been noted theologians. Some have been dishwashers. Some have been ditch diggers. Some have raised families. Some have built solid businesses.

Some have found wisdom in hard ways, walking through many valleys of the shadow. Some have come upon wisdom gently enough, as though, on a pleasant, cool, not too warm day. All of them have discovered good friends in humility and wisdom.

HUMILITY AND WISDOM

Live with humility and wisdom. You will live in the grace of God.

One key, one possibility, for a whole, healthy life is the mutual gift of humility and wisdom. God invites us to a life of humility, not arrogance. God invites us to a life of wisdom, not confusion. Wisdom is more than data and demographics, graphs and charts. Wisdom is more than calculations and rationalities. We grow forward in life when, amidst the confusions, chaos, and competing claims that abound, we discover the resources for wisdom in our lives by developing:

- A sense of humility, of meekness before the truth
- The benefit of helpful mentors
- A sense of vision for our life
- Common sense in living life

God invites us to a life of humility and wisdom. Humility is the first step toward wisdom. We are at our best when, amidst the perplexities and puzzles around us, we discover the resources for a life of humility and wisdom.

It impresses me that genuine experts in any field have both a quiet confidence, a steady, unassuming assurance for what they do know, and a deep, abiding meekness for what they have yet to learn. Wisdom lacks arrogance. Wisdom is not pompous. Wisdom does not boast. The beginning of wisdom is meekness, humility.

God comes to us directly. God comes to us in Jesus Christ. God comes to us in the Spirit. God comes to us in our mentors. God helps us discover wise mentors to help us grow forward in this life. Our lives have a sense of confidence and assurance, a deep, abiding resource for living as we sense the presence of our mentors with us. Our lives benefit from the mentors who have helped us in the past and who are helping us now.

We discover these words in Hebrews:

Hebrews 12:1

"Wherefore, seeing we also are compassed about
with so great a cloud of witnesses . . ."

Picture a stadium full of witnesses—a stadium larger than any we have yet to build in this sector of the galaxies. The witnesses are our mentors, encouragers, coaches, the people who encourage us, cheer us on, who wish for us the best, and who help us live life at our best. With our mentors, wisdom comes.

We lead healthy lives as we have a sense of vision for our lives. Vision is about more than a misplaced preoccupation as to whether we are going to survive or not. If we reduce our vision for our lives to our survival, we do not even survive. We are already dead.

So many of the so-called vision statements boil down to a statement calling for the institutional survival of some organization. The statements focus on trying to do something to ensure the organization will lose no more members than it already has lost. The effort is to stop the decline. The goal is to try to get more new members in order to slow down or stop the decline.

Vision has to do with life, not institutionalism. Vision has to do with mission, with serving persons in their lives and destinies. It has to do with shepherding persons with their human hurts and hopes. Vision has to do with wonder and joy, justice and peace. Vision grows out of compassion, humility, and wisdom.

Say to yourself, "I have this vision for my life." Then, go on to describe the sense of vision you see as important for your life. We do want our lives to count. We do want to lead lives of meaning and value, purpose and significance. We do want to make some difference. Our sense of vision helps us do so.

Vision is rooted in what counts—at the end. Martin Luther King, Jr. expressed his vision for his life and mission in his speech, "I Have a Dream." Vision recognizes that some things—not all things—are of value in this life. What counts has to do with human hurts and people's hopes. Wisdom helps us discern what is genuinely important in our lives.

Wisdom is not grandiose and flamboyant. Wisdom is not lofty and arrogant. Wisdom is down to earth. God invites us to use our best common sense. Wisdom and common sense are good friends.

Someone once said, "If common sense were that common, more people would have it." I do think common sense is common. Common sense is more common than people believe. Many people simply do not consciously draw forward and claim what, in fact, they intuitively know.

Thousands of times, people have come to me at the close of a seminar and said things like, "Thank you. What you have shared makes sense. As we listened, we realized we knew what you were teaching us. We simply didn't know we knew." Or, "As you were talking, it dawned on me that I knew what you were sharing. I just didn't realize I did." Or, "I appreciate your helping us discover what we knew—and now know we knew." Given half a chance, most people have the capacity for common sense.

For a whole, healthy life, it is helpful that you live with humility and wisdom.

This is the time to gather our best thinking, our thoughtful discernment. This is the time to discover our deepest understanding of life, so that we can make some sense of the time God gives us. This is the time for meekness, mentors, vision, and common sense. With these resources we discover humility and wisdom to live our lives richly and fully.

Where persons live humility and wisdom, there is the grace of God.

Prayer

Living God, we are grateful for the wonder of your universe, the majesty of your creation, and the power of your grace. We are humbly thankful for being alive, for the gifts of compassion and wisdom. We live with love and hope, joy and wonder. We pray we may be worthy of the trust you have placed with us. May our lives count well for your cause.

With the grace of God, we pray.

Amen.

10. JUST ENOUGH HELP

Dorothy, the Samaritan, and the Innkeeper

We share just enough help.
We live in the grace of God.

A decisive event in my own life is my discovery of how much help is really helpful. The decisive persons are Dorothy, the Samaritan, and the Innkeeper.

Dorothy would call late at night or very early in the morning. There were a whole series of Saturday mornings when she would call and say something like this, "I'm in the bathroom. The razor blades are on the counter. I can't take it anymore. I'm just calling to say goodbye."

Her phone call would cause me to talk her through the crisis till sunrise, or, while Julie held the fort on the phone, I would rush over to help. These were not "wolf, wolf, wolf" phone calls. They were dead serious. Dorothy knew how to slash her wrists correctly to make it to the other side of the river, and she had nearly done so three times.

I finally figured out her fear: it was chaos. Many of us are fearful of chaos. Her work, her job delivered her sufficient structure that she could make it through the week. But Friday at five o'clock in the afternoon, she entered a world of chaos, a world of no structure. By early Saturday morning, with her fears, her anxieties, her apprehensions, her nervousness, her tenseness, her worries, her terror of chaos, she was ready to call this world quits.

I began to phone her at work on Friday morning, at her ten o'clock break. She, with a sheet of paper and a pencil, and I with a sheet of paper and a pencil, together would structure her weekend. Whom she would see. Where. When. What she would do. We put together a detailed schedule that organized her time from five o'clock Friday afternoon until early Saturday morning. Then we put in place, in detail, the schedule for all of Saturday and Sunday as well.

It worked.

Then, it didn't. Then, it did. It didn't. It did. It didn't. It did. It didn't.

Then, it did and did and did.

Some years went by. Dorothy called. She had been transferred several years before to another city. She was coming through town and hoped we could visit together over lunch. She wanted to thank me for all those times I had talked her through to sunrise, and for all those times I had rushed over. Most especially, she wanted to thank me for the ten-minute phone calls on Friday mornings.

She said to me, "I want you to know that it was in those Friday morning ten-minute phone calls that I began to learn how to take control of my life. I learned how to lead my own life."

One key, one possibility, for a whole, healthy life is discovering just enough help for leading your own life. God invites us to *lead* our lives, not simply react to what life brings us. We are at our best when, amidst the chaos, the excesses, the loss of power, and the conflicts that abound, we develop the resources for leading our lives.

We discover how to give ourselves just enough help to be helpful. Our tendency, when seeking to help others, is to give too much help. Our tendency, when seeking to help ourselves, is to give ourselves too much help. The art is to give just enough help. We will lead solid and helpful lives.

Dorothy helped me to learn to share just enough help, but not too much help. I was thinking of Dorothy one day. Julie and I were glad to have heard recently from her. She had sent us a note. She had shared in her note that she was thriving and doing well.

The scripture I was studying that week was the text of the Good Samaritan.

Thinking of Dorothy, and studying the text, a new understanding of the parable came to me. On Sunday, in the sermon, I shared the text found in Luke 10:30–37 and my newfound understanding. This is part of what I shared in the sermon.

Luke 10:30–37

And Jesus answering said,
"A certain man went down from Jerusalem to Jericho and
fell among thieves, which stripped him of his raiment, and
wounded him, and departed, leaving him half dead.

And by chance there came down a certain priest that way,
And when he saw him, he passed by on the other side.

And likewise a Levite, when he was at the place,
came and looked on him, and passed on the other side.

But a certain Samaritan, as he journeyed, came where he was,
and when he saw him; he had compassion on him.

And went to him, and bound up his wounds,

pouring in oil and wine, and set him on his own beast,
and brought him to an inn, and took care of him.

And on the morrow when he departed,
he took out two pence, and gave them to the host, and said,
Take care of him;
and whatsoever thou spendest more,
when I come again, I will repay thee.

Which now of these three,
thinkest thou, was neighbor unto him that fell among the thieves?

And he said, He that shewed mercy on him,
Then said Jesus unto him, "Go and do thou likewise.

A hushed stillness had settled across the land. The cooling evening breezes were like a welcoming friend. It had been a long, hard day. There were many travelers on the road. The inn was full. His grandfather had started the inn. His father had enlarged the kitchen. He had built the business.

Two window shutters to close, three candles to snuff, and it would be time to go to bed. A faint knock on the door, barely heard. It came again. Who could that be at this time of night? He went slowly to the door and opened it.

A man stood before him. The man was dressed like a Samaritan. Behind him stood a donkey with a rumpled clump of clothing on its back. The pile of clothing slipped slowly to the ground as the innkeeper watched. Then, from the ground came a moan. The Samaritan told the innkeeper that he had found the man by the side of the road, beaten and robbed, and that he had brought him to the inn for help. Could the innkeeper help?

It is interesting to think of the possibilities available to the innkeeper. He could have said, "There is no room in the inn. I cannot help."

He could have taken the man in, taken advantage of the Samaritan's generosity, and given more help than was really needed. The Samaritan had said, "Whatever it costs, I will pay you on my return." The innkeeper could have seen his dream of the condominium on the Sea of Galilee finally coming true.

The innkeeper could have refused to help or he could have given too much help. The innkeeper chose neither of these alternatives.

What the Samaritan and the innkeeper did was to take the man in and help him just enough so that the man could be on his way. There is nothing in the text that suggests the innkeeper delivered so much help that, out of gratitude and gratefulness, the beaten and robbed man lived, lo, the rest of his days with the innkeeper. That would have been a dependent and co-dependent pattern of behavior.

JUST ENOUGH HELP

Share just enough help. You will live in the grace of God.

We want to help. We deliver too much help. We create dependent and co-dependent patterns of behavior. Helpful people have a tendency to deliver more help than is helpful.

The genius of the parable is that the passerby least likely to stop, the Samaritan, was the one who did stop. There is nothing in the parable that suggests he first ponders, thinks, considers, and weighs the consequences. For him, it is simply a generous, spontaneous act of help and kindness.

The genius of the parable is that the innkeeper gave just enough help. The genius of the parable is that the man was able to be on his way.

We long for some mission where we can be directly involved. We are happy to give generous money. What we want to do is give generous, direct help. We want to participate in sharing specific, concrete help. We want to share more than good intentions, glowing generalities, and syrupy sentimentalities. We want our help to be genuinely helpful.

The art of helping is to share just enough help to be helpful.

In the parable of the Samaritan and the innkeeper, this is what happens. The Samaritan delivers just enough help to get the man, beaten and robbed, to the inn. The innkeeper delivers just enough help that the man, now restored, can be on his journey. The art of helping is to share just enough help to be helpful, but not so much help that the help becomes harmful and creates a pattern of dependency and codependency.

The Samaritan did not go back to the place on the road where the man was beaten and robbed and set up a booth to help all persons beaten and robbed for the years to come. The innkeeper did not lavish so much help on the man, month after month, year after year, that, out of gratitude and gratefulness, the man lived, lo, the rest of his days with the innkeeper.

We learn this from the parable. God delivers just enough help to us so that we can be on our journey.

Sometimes, the grace of God comes to us in the form of a Samaritan, sometimes in the form of an innkeeper. We learn to share just enough help with others and with ourselves. We learn not to overhelp others or overhelp ourselves.

God shares with us acts of spontaneous grace and generosity, mercy and kindness, joy and peace, with just enough help, so that we can be on our journey through this life.

Share just enough help. Live in the grace of God.

Where persons share just enough help, there is the grace of God.

Prayer

Almighty and Everlasting God, we are grateful for the wondrous help that you give to us. With generosity, you give us just enough help that we can be on the journey of this life. Help us to be as helpful as you are. Help us to resist giving too much help. Help us to avoid the pitfall of creating co-dependent and dependent patterns of relationships. Help our helping to be just enough help.

With the grace of God, we pray.

Amen.

11. TWO FOR ONE

Gene and Bob

We live two for one.
We live in the grace of God.

A decisive event in my own life is a consultation I shared with a congregation. The two decisive persons are Gene and Bob.

I was helping a given congregation. Gene and I were visiting on my first day there, in the afternoon. The sunlight was streaming through the windows, on one of those remarkably beautiful days we cherish in life.

Gene is one of the central leaders in the church. He and his carpentry team built the original sanctuary, now used as their chapel. Next, he and his construction company built the Christian education building. Importantly, he and his building firm then went on to build the new sanctuary, one of the finest in the region.

The congregation is part of a denomination that historically had not allowed women to vote on congregational matters. Many years before, at the national level of the denomination, a new policy had been adopted, namely, that women could vote—potentially. It was left to each individual congregation to decide the matter for itself.

Gene said to me, "Dr. Callahan, I see our congregation as an island in the lake." Translation: All the other churches in that denomination in that community had, in recent times, individually decided women could vote on congregational matters. Gene's church had not. In his view, his congregation was upholding the historic tradition of the past.

I said, "Gene, either the island is sinking, or the water is rising, and you and I had better build a bridge to the mainland, or find us a boat, before we are the last ones left on this island as it sinks." We talked long that afternoon.

Bob had come as pastor six years before. He favored women voting. He was considered a liberal in the denomination. In the late spring at the end of his first year there, he called a congregational meeting to decide whether women could vote. Gene gathered people out of the woodwork to defeat the proposal.

Gene won by several votes.

The next year, and for five consecutive years, Bob called for a vote each spring, and each of the five times Gene gathered people out of the woodwork to defeat the proposal. Their liturgical year had become Christmas, Easter, The Vote. And, the most recent vote had happened two weeks before my arrival. There was still lots of heat and fire left around.

The second day there, Bob and I were headed to a meeting in his car. As we were driving along, I said to Bob:

"I have a puzzle. You were here as pastor six months when your secretary said it would be helpful to her if the bulletin could be done on Thursday rather than on Friday. Your response was, 'I have always done the bulletin on Friday, and I don't plan to change now.'

"Time passed. She asked again. And again, your response was, 'I have always done the bulletin on Friday, and I don't plan to change now.'

"Over the six years come and gone, she has asked on yet a few more occasions.

"Recently, she and the personnel committee together requested the possibility of the bulletin being done on Thursday rather than Friday. Your entrenched response was, 'I have always done the bulletin on Friday, and I don't plan to change now.'

"You shared much of this with me yesterday.

"Bob, I have a puzzle. On something as simple as the bulletin being done on Thursday or Friday, your response is, 'I have always done the bulletin on Friday, and I don't plan to change now.'

"On something major and foundational to the historic identity of this congregation, your message is, 'Please change now.'

"Help me understand this puzzle."

There was a long, long silence. We rode two whole blocks. We sat at a long traffic light. There was yet more silence.

Finally, Bob said, "I see what you mean."

"Bob," I said, "I have another puzzle. You teach me—your congregation teaches me—that your best preaching happens on Sunday night. You study the text. You consult the commentaries. You pray for your message. With a simple outline, you share a warm, insightful, encouraging sermon. Your people leave with what I call handles of help and hope.

"On Sunday morning, you virtually read a long, tedious manuscript sermon. Both you and your people teach me that your preaching on Sunday evening is most helpful."

"For you, from now on, Sunday morning is Sunday evening."

"Each Sunday morning, feel free to share the best Sunday evening sermon you can. And if, on Sunday evening, you read your beloved manuscript sermon, it won't do that much damage and harm. There aren't that many people there anyway."

That day, I suggested to Bob that he make these two changes in himself, simply and quietly. I suggested that he not announce that, from this day forward, the bulletin would be done on Thursday, not Friday. I suggested he simply begin the practice, gently and quietly, of giving his secretary the bulletin on Thursday.

Likewise, he could simply begin, on a given Sunday morning, sharing a helpful Sunday evening sermon. It would help for him to not make much to-do about the matter. I suggested to him that people would sense his own flexibility and growth.

I encouraged him not to set up a bargain—namely, his saying he would make these two changes if women would be allowed to vote. Bargaining would not help. What would help, what would give his people confidence and assurance that they could change, was that they would sense his own willingness to change, to be flexible.

Some time passed. As I remember, ten to twelve weeks came and went after I had shared with the congregation. Gene called me long distance, just before Julie and I were to leave for Australia. He said, "Dr. Callahan, would it really work for women to vote in our congregation?"

I said, "Yes, Gene, it will work, and you will be remembered years hence as the person who built the original sanctuary, which is now the chapel, the education building, and the new sanctuary. Most especially, fifty years from now, you will be remembered as the person who built the bridge to the mainland."

Then, I said, "Gene, you will want to deal with the ghost of your mother in some other way." Ghost of mother. I always ask myself, when someone expends as much energy as Gene had over five years, gathering people out of the woodwork to defeat a proposal, what more is going on here than is apparent?

The reason we had talked long and late that first afternoon is because we were talking about his growing-up years. He was the oldest of four. He was seven years old when his father deserted the family. His mother took her anger, bitterness, and resentment out on her oldest son.

From the time he was seven until he became fifteen, she beat him up, emotionally, physically, spiritually. When he got to be fifteen he was big enough to beat her up, but rather than do that, he ran away from home, got a job as a carpenter's helper, and worked himself up over the years to his own major building firm.

I said, "Gene, you will want to deal with the ghost of your mother in some other way. It is not fair to her. It is not fair to you. It is not fair to the congregation you dearly love."

Three things happen in that congregation today.

One, the bulletin is done on Thursday.

Two, every Sunday morning, Bob preaches the best Sunday evening sermon in the area. His sermons help.

Three, women vote.

TWO FOR ONE

Make two changes in yourself. You will live in the grace of God.

It was in helping Gene and Bob's congregation that I discovered the learning I call two for one: *Make two changes in yourself for each one change you hope for in other persons.*

We want other people to change. When I lead seminars on leadership, the most frequent, compelling question in the grouping is, "Dr. Callahan, how can we get the people in our congregation to change?" Both key leaders and pastors ask this question. Their primary interest is in helping other people to change.

This was Bob's question of me.

It came to me that, if only one person could change, it could be Bob. Likewise, in any grouping of which you are a part, if only one person can change, it is you. If you can only lead one person, lead yourself. Leadership begins at home—with you. You have more influence over yourself than you do over anyone else.

When you develop the capacity to lead yourself, you grow forward the capacity to lead others. Someone who cannot lead themselves has grave difficulty in leading others. You practice leadership, first, with yourself. You, first, grow forward yourself.

We have had the joy of having many wonderful pets across the years. We have had great fun going to obedience classes, some with the best trainers in the country. With the best trainers, the focus is on helping the leader of the pet learn how to be the leader. The training class is more for the pet owner than for the pet. When you have developed the capacity to lead yourself, then, and only then, will you be able to lead your pet.

Indeed, the focus in the class is on helping the person learn how to develop a mutual relationship with his or her dog. Frequently, the dog learns more quickly than the owner. The trainer invests most of the time in training the owner to be a competent leader. This encourages the owner to make many changes in one's behavior and spirit.

In AA, the focus is on helping the recovering alcoholic to learn how to lead his or her own behavior. No one does the recovery steps for the person. No one "makes the changes" for the person. The recovering alcoholic works the twelve-step program. The AA sponsor is there to coach the person as they recover. The sponsor is not there to do the program for them.

With groupings of people, whether families, interest groups, or congregations, it is decisive that leaders achieve the changes in themselves first. They make these changes in themselves with compassion and wisdom. AA sponsors made the changes in themselves; they work their own twelve-step program *before* they become sponsors. Changing, growing persons can coach changing, growing persons.

We do not do two changes in ourselves as a bargain so that those around us will make one change in themselves. "Bargain change" does not work. It reduces the matter to a "tit for tat" negotiation. It reduces the relationship to law. What helps is grace. The art is to illustrate, with confidence and assurance, one's own capacity for change, for growing forward one of these: a new behavior, a new spirit, a new insight, a new pattern.

Change encourages change. When you change, in two simple ways, it gives people around you the confidence and assurance that they, too, can change. Change is contagious. People develop confidence and let go of fear. People develop assurance and let go of old habits. Feel free to change—to grow yourself forward.

Where persons live two for one, there is the grace of God.

Prayer

*Everlasting God, we are grateful you give us the
encouragement to change and to grow. We are thankful
for your confidence and assurance with us. We are who
we are because of your grace. We will be who we are
becoming because of your hope. You lead us forward.
Forgive our faltering and hesitation, our worry and
anxious spirit. Grant us your courage for the days
to come. Help us to trust in your grace and peace.*

With the grace of God, we pray.

Amen.

12. LIVE HOPE

John and Mary

We live hope.
We live in the grace of God.

A decisive event in my own life happened late one night. The two decisive persons are John and Mary.

In the middle of the night, our phone rang. It was a woman on the other end of the line—upset, confused, babbling, blurting disconnected sentences, near hysteria. I could hardly understand what she was saying.

As best I could make it out, her husband had come home. Words had been exchanged. Pushing and shoving had occurred. He had begun beating on her. She had broken away and locked herself in the bedroom, and made a hurried call. Would I come?

I was naive in those days and said yes. Today, in comparably desperate circumstances, I am naive still and say yes still. There was some considerable credibility to the desperation of her plea because I could hear this banging in the background, as though someone were knocking on or breaking down a bedroom door.

It took me ten minutes to get to the road on which they lived. As I turned down the road, the thing that struck me the most—I can see it now—was pitch darkness. Not a light on anywhere up or down that road; not a street light, not a front yard light, not a porch light, not a light on in any house, save the house toward which I was headed. And, early that morning, every light in the house must have been on.

There was fog, and you know how the light shimmers out across a fog. It gave me a kind of eerie feeling as I parked my car and rushed to the door. The closer I got to the half-open front door, the less interested I was in achieving the door. I could hear the hollering and yelling, screaming and shouting in the back of the house.

I did the wise, sensible thing that any competent minister would do under those desperate circumstances. I rang the doorbell. I rang it again. Surely, these people will hear their doorbell, interrupt whatever they are doing in the back of the house, and come gently, politely, decently to answer the bell and say, "Why, Pastor, what a delight that you are sharing a pastoral visit with us at two in the morning."

They would invite me in for coffee or tea. We would have a pleasant twenty-minute visit, and I would never have to be a part of whatever mess was going on in their lives early that morning. I was so confident of that strategy that I knocked on the doorjamb. Maybe they hadn't heard the bell. I couldn't knock on the door, standing half-ajar. If I had knocked on it, I would have knocked it back against the wall. So I knocked on the doorjamb.

Then, much to my horror and dismay, I found my feet carrying me down the hall toward the noise. I said to my feet, "Let's go back and try that doorbell one more time. Sometimes you have to push them really hard."

I went down the hall, turned to the right, then back to the left, and entered their family room. I just followed the shouting to know where they were.

Mary was strewn across the couch, her nightdress torn, blood streaming from the side of her mouth, bruises black and blue beginning to appear on her face. She was indeed having a hard morning.

Her husband was standing over by the fireplace, shouting and yelling, screaming and hollering, making noise that reached to the high heavens, filling that room with more anger, hatred, and hostility than likely all of us could muster in a year's time.

He turned to see what stranger had walked into his own home in the middle of the night. Stranger. They were not members of our church. They were newcomers in our community. One afternoon, late, I had visited to welcome them as part of the community. Mary had been there. He had not been there.

My custom with newcomer families across the years has been to invite them to put my phone number on the front of their telephone directory. That is where most newcomers keep track of phone numbers they would almost like to remember but cannot quite, yet. I would rather be the penciled phone number on the front of the phone directory than the institutional calling card, now on the dresser, then on the ironing board, and lost a week later.

For whatever reasons, when Mary broke away from her husband, headed into the bedroom, closed and locked the bedroom door, and rushed to the phone, rather than calling the police, she had seen that penciled phone number and called me. He and I had never met.

When he turned to see what stranger had just walked into his own home amidst the chaos and confusion he was creating, I noticed for the first time that he was holding in his arm—just the way John Wayne used to hold those things in the movies—he was holding in his arm a semiautomatic submachine gun.

There was in me, in one split second, an eternity of sheer terror. I can feel it now.

There was also a side of me that said, "By golly, he doesn't use that for deer hunting. He probably doesn't use it for duck hunting. He wouldn't use it for target shooting. He would obliterate the targets."

I am a reasonably wise, sensible person.

It dawned on me as I stood there in sheer terror that what I said next might very well be decisive for me, and for Mary—and, I learned later, for three little kids huddled in a back bedroom, their door closed, sort of tucked under their bed, wondering what in the name of heaven mommy and daddy were doing early that morning, and not very interested in finding out.

I said, "John." I caught him just a little.

As best as I can in this life's pilgrimage, I believe in living it through with people on a first-name basis. In that hurried, confused, near-hysteria telephone call, Mary had described her husband, John, as having come home and begun beating on her. Since it sounded like he and I were at last going to meet, I had remembered his name.

Here was John seeing a total stranger, walking into his own home early that morning, amidst all of the disturbance and commotion he was creating, and calling him by his first name. I caught his attention just a little.

I said, "John, where are you headed?
What kind of future are you building this morning?"

Those two questions caught John just long enough that we could begin a four-hour conversation that eventuated in a five-year relationship as John and Mary and their three kids, myself, and a host of others helped them to build forward a rich and full future.

John had come home from his own fair share of carousing and carrying-on. He had found his wife, Mary, in her own fair share of carousing and carrying-on. The neighbor had gotten away. Out of his guilt over what he had been about, and out of his anger over what he had found in his home, and most especially out of his terror, he had been shouting to the high heavens.

Terror.

Take away a person's memories, and he becomes anxious. Take away a person's hopes, and he becomes terrified.

When John walked into his own home early that morning and found what he found, whatever hopes he had for himself, whatever hopes he had for himself and Mary, whatever hopes he had for himself and Mary and their three kids, whatever hopes he had for this life's pilgrimage, were smashed to smithereens around his feet. The door to the future had been slammed shut in his face.

He could see no way forward.

To be sure, he was shouting his guilt and his anger. Most especially, early that morning, he was shouting his terror to the high heavens.

Those two questions, "John, where are you heading? What kind of future are you building this morning?" opened the door to the future just enough of a crack that we could begin that four-hour conversation and develop that five-year relationship.

Don't get too caught up in the gun.

By that time, having worked in a mission with alcoholics and their families, I had successfully gotten myself beaten up three times and seen my share of knives, handguns, and one shotgun. Bizarre events happen in the best of families, especially when people are struggling with alcoholism.

Now, to be sure, early that morning was the first time I had found myself standing in front of a semiautomatic submachine gun. Once in a lifetime is enough. I've had my turn. But don't get too caught up in the gun.

Decisive events change our lives and shape our destinies. The most decisive event of that morning was my discovery of those two questions.

If I had asked the question that I had been *taught* to ask in seminary, I would have said, "John, what's the problem?" There is considerable probability John might have spewed his problems all over the family room early that morning. Whether Mary or I or their three little kids or John—or any or all of us—would be here yet today is open to some considerable conjecture.

LIVE HOPE

Live hope. You will live in the grace of God.

I don't know where those two questions came from, save God. They were not a part of my own perspective, my own way of thinking, my own frame of reference. They were not the way I had been looking at life. I would have said, "John, what's the problem?"

Only something as dramatic as that event and as drastic as that gun, could shake me from my old, well-ingrained habit of "what is the problem?" to discover these two new questions.

The gift of grace of that morning was my discovery of these two questions of hope. The questions Where are you headed? and What kind of future are you building? are questions that confirm one can head somewhere, that there is a future toward which one can head. They are questions that look forward. They are questions of hope and grace.

In that early morning time, over our four hours of conversation, John still had the gun. From time to time, the gun wavered my way and Mary's, and the sense of sheer terror returned. It was now six o'clock. The sun was coming up. I could see we were making progress, and we were going to get beyond the mess of that morning.

And, we had gotten about as far as we were going to get for that morning.

My curiosity got the better of me, and I asked, "John, where did you get the gun?"

He told me he had bought the gun earlier that year to protect his wife and his family.

I said, "John, you've spent the last four hours pointing the gun you bought to protect your wife and family at both your wife and your pastor."

Now, they were not members of our church. And, I am perfectly willing to claim to be someone's pastor when he needs the help of a pastor, and early that morning it looked to me like John needed all the help a pastor could give.

So I said, "John, you've spent the last four hours pointing the gun you bought to protect your wife and your family at both your wife and your pastor. Now, put it down, so we can get about the business of building the future."

And he did. And we did.

Hope is strong. Look for hope. You will find it.

Discover where you are headed. You will live in the grace of God.

Live hope. You will live in the grace of God.

Hope is stronger than memory. Memory is strong. Hope is stronger. People live on hope more than memory. Take away a person's memories and they become anxious. Take away a person's hopes and they become terrified.

Anxiety yields fear. Fear yields anger. Anger yields rage. These four—anxiety, fear, anger, rage—go together and reinforce one another. Fortunately, grace, hope, confidence, and assurance are stronger. When we live hope, we live in the grace of God.

Where persons live hope, there is the grace of God.

Prayer

Almighty and Everloving God, we are grateful for the hope you give to us. We are amazed at the generosity of your grace in our lives. When we forget, help us to remember. When we become lost, help us to find our way. When we become troubled and anxious, still our spirit. Give us a spirit of calm, a sense of peace, a joy and wonder for life. Help us to live hope in our lives.

With the grace of God, we pray.

Amen.

II

Ways to Study
and Apply the
Learnings

GROWING FORWARD

Living in the grace of God is a joyous, encouraging way of living. We discover happiness and hope, wonder and peace. The foregoing monograph has value and integrity in its own right. Each of the twelve decisive events has been of central importance in my own life. I am who I am, in major part, because of these events, and their being filled with the grace of God.

Along the way I have discovered four possibilities for growing forward our own learnings and our own experiencing of the grace of God.

1. MATCHING EVENTS

Think of matching events in your own life that stir one of these learnings:

compassion

claiming strengths

having fun

valuing excellent mistakes

building on your strengths

living progress

letting go

running with compassion

humility and wisdom

just enough help

two for one

living hope

As you think of your life, you will discover matching events in your own life that stir these learnings, these experiences of grace.

I encourage you to develop the memory, the sense, and the spirit of comparable events that have been decisive for you. Remember and relive these decisive events of grace. They have happened in your life so you can experience the grace of God.

Likewise, I encourage you to anticipate future events that stir your experiences of grace in any of these twelve learnings. Our anticipation of the grace of God gives us hope for God's grace in our lives. We are who we are because decisive events, filled with the grace of God, have come to us. We are who we are because we look forward to decisive events that advance our experiences of grace.

You are welcome to gather a group of friends and family.

Select one of the twelve learnings in this book. Share in reading the chapter aloud. Or, you can each read the chapter ahead of the gathering.

Then, go around the circle. Encourage each person to share a similar event. It could be an event from one's own life, or from the life a family member or friend. It could be an event from the Bible. It could from history, or from literature, or from recent events.

The sharing of comparable events will encourage all. The sharing of similar events will help all to experience the grace of God. We will learn from one another and from our shared experiences of grace.

2. THIS ONE DAY

Practice one of the twelve learnings this one day.

I want to share a word on behalf of *this one day*. Live *this one day* in the grace of God. These twelve learnings are decisive and helpful for living a whole, healthy life in the grace of God. Feel free to practice one of these twelve learnings *this one day*. Select a day. Pick a day. Practice a specific learning for *this one day*.

In a real sense, we can only live *this one day*. Yesterday is gone. Tomorrow is yet to be. We are given today, *this one day*. We can grow forward our learnings and our experiencing of the grace of God *this one day*.

Some groupings suggest that the idea should be to focus on *every day*. Their thought is that one must discipline one's self to a rigorous routine of the daily practice of all twelve learnings *every day*. Or, at the very least, one must practice *one* of the twelve learnings *every day*.

I find that approach to be an example of compulsive addictive perfectionism. Such a preoccupied perfectionism is not grace.

Feel free to not practice all twelve learnings *every day*.

Feel free to not practice one learning *every day*.

Look down the list of the twelve learnings. Select one you would have fun practicing for *this one day*. You are not signing up for every day, or even every other day. You are having fun sharing a best practice of this one learning for *this one day*.

Live your compassion	Julie
Claim your strengths	Bobby
Have fun	Marie and Jason and the Great Banquet
Value excellent mistakes	The Coral Reef
Build on your strengths	Harold and Steve
Live progress	Sweet Silence and Hilda Mae
Let go	The Slipping Anchor
Compassion runs	The Running Fathe
Humility and wisdom	Dr. Politella

Just enough help	Dorothy, the Samaritan, the Innkeeper
Two for one	Gene and Bob
Live hope	John and Mary

Yes, select a day. Select one of the twelve learnings. Practice this learning for *this one day*. Have fun. Discover you can do it for *this one day*. Give thanks to God.

Live, *this one day*, in the grace of God.

The art is to select *this one day* and *this one learning* and have fun living in the grace of God for *this one day*.

Select another day. Select another of the twelve learnings. Explore this learning for this day. Practice this learning for this one day. Live, *this one day*, in the grace of God. Give thanks to God.

3. SPILLOVER IMPACT

Count on Spillover Impact.

Grace spills over. Grace cannot be contained. Grace is joyous and abundant, overflowing and bursting at the seams. Grow forward your practice of some of these twelve learnings from easy to difficult.

You can count on spillover impact among the twelve learnings. The spirit is to discover which of the twelve learnings you would have fun exploring and practicing. Select three that are natural and are easy for you. Do not start with the hardest, for you, of the twelve.

Build on your strengths. Develop a spirit of rhythm, of spillover impact. Grow forward one to three of the twelve. The others will come.

Think of the twelve in sets of three. These three are natural and easy for you. Then, you can have fun with three that are a little more advanced. In time, you will have fun practicing the three that are, in fact, advanced. Then, you can be at peace about the three that, for you, are difficult. You can head toward nine of the twelve.

You are welcome to never focus on all twelve. Think of the twelve learnings in this ascending order:

Natural and easy these three

A little more advanced   these three

Advanced   these three

Difficult   these three

Grow forward the three that are easy and, then, the three that are a little more advanced. Again, I suggest you not start with the ones that are hardest for you. Begin with your strengths. Begin where you have experienced the grace of God the deepest and the richest.

Certainly, you can select one of the twelve learnings and have fun practicing it for, perhaps, a few days in a row. Note that I suggest, at most, a few days. You can always come back to that one later on. Do not try to practice it for days on end, "until you get it right." You are not trying for perfectionism. I am encouraging you to have fun exploring, now here, now there, some of these twelve learnings.

There will come a time when some of these learnings become so natural and spontaneous that you no longer "think" about them. They simply happen. They have become part of you. They are you.

You are not trying to develop all twelve to perfection. You are not trying to develop absolutes of behavior. You are growing forward some of these learnings as you experience living in the grace of God.

4. LEARNINGS

**Grow forward your learnings of grace in the same ways
you grow forward any area of your life.**

The gift of this book is to share these twelve decisive events, grace-filled, and the learnings that have helped me in my own life. These decisive events have given me a richer, fuller under-standing of the grace of God. These twelve learnings are "best practices" for living in the grace of God. I commend these twelve to you.

The further gift of this book is the insight that we can practice these twelve learnings as keys to living a whole, healthy life in the grace of God. We can live these possibilities, these learnings, and these best practices one at a time, now here, now there, as we feel led by the Spirit of God.

Trust yourself. Trust your creativity and flexibility. Trust your own heart and imagination. Develop a structure of learnings that works for you. There is no "one way" to learn something. There are multiple possibilities.

Learn some of these twelve learnings in the same ways you have fun learning in any area of your life.

The art is to explore and discover, with your creativity, how you best grow forward your learnings. In music, we pick up the instrument and begin to explore the notes. We play the instrument, experimentally and improvisationally. We listen for the rhythm, melody, and tune.

In art, we discover the canvas and the paints. We experiment. We try this and that. We innovate. We create. We explore tex-ture and color. We stumble into the color wheel of balance and contrast. We discover a rhythm of design, shape, and colors that matches with us.

In cooking, we do the same. We explore the tastes and the flavors. We have fun with the appearance and presentation. We develop the consistency and texture. We add this or that condi-ment. We bake, fry, microwave, cool, and heat. We innovate. We have fun. We are creative.

In quilting, we explore the patterns, the textures, the color com-binations, and the designs. We create quilts that express our feelings—our passions—our loves. We honor persons, groupings, and events. We remember wonderful times in our history. We anticipate wonderful times in our future.

In sports, we look at the plays, the combinations of players, the speed, the quickness, and the timing. We consider the strategies, the checks and balances, the offenses and the defenses. We think of the patterns, the precedents, and the possibilities.

In writing, we draw on the creativity of the words, the passages, the descriptions, the phrases, and the content. We think of the plot, the humor, the tragedy, the narrative, the poetry of the story. We confirm the oral traditions in the written word.

In construction, architecture, or ditch digging, we do the same. Form, structure, design, and color are creative possibilities for our projects. Blueprints, models, outlines, and archetypes are our guides.

In many, many ways and in many, many areas of life, we anticipate and advance. We explore and innovate. We are creative and inventive. We are ingenious and imaginative. We are original and resourceful. We are inspired and inspire.

Think of an area of your life where you are creative. In a spirit comparable to this area, now, select one learning among the twelve you would have fun growing in your life. Grow this learning forward with the same creative spirit. You will have fun. You will grow forward. You will advance your gifts for living in the grace of God.

BEST PRACTICES

I encourage you to grow forward your learnings in ways that match with whom you are and who you are heading to becoming. You can grow forward in any of the following eight ways you would have fun exploring.

Spontaneous
One day
Week end
Work week
Whole week
Twelve days
Monthly
Seasonal

There is a sense in which this list is from shorter to longer. The length of the duration moves from a shorter to a longer period of time.

The art is to learn the learning, not the length. There is no merit in longer. We are not trying to go from shorter to longer. The art is to practice the learning so we can learn the learning, not so we can do it longer.

As I observed in my book, *The Future That Has Come*, in 2002, some of us have learned the behavior pattern of excellent sprint-ers. We do what we do in short term, highly intensive ways near the time at hand. Some of us have learned the behavior pattern of solid marathon runners. We do what we do in routine, regular ways, weekly, monthly, year round.

Many of us have learned both patterns of behavior. We can chose which pattern of behavior is helpful and appropriate for a given setting.

I began my research and lecturing on these patterns of behavior in 1993. I had brought my research to a solid point of publishing the results in 2002. Since then, during these past ten years, I have continued to advance my research.

There is a tendency among solid marathon runners to assume the longer one does something the better one becomes at it. The art is to experience the grace, to discover the learning, not to do it longer. Focus on the grace, not the length.

Any of the eight possibilities for Best Practices are helpful. Select the ones that help you to grow forward the learning, to experience the grace. There is no one way to grow forward. Some people insist that the one way they have done it is the only way it can be done. They develop an autocratic, dictatorial spirit. They insist that their way is "the way."

The truth is that there are many ways people grow forward. The art is to discover the variety of ways that work for you. At a given point in time, "the grace of grace" is that you can grow and develop the learnings of grace in multiple ways. Your creativity, flexibility, and discovery will help you find the ways that help you grow you.

Finally, only you can grow you. No one can grow you for you. And, only you can discover the ways you can grow you. People can share their wisdom and experience, their achievements and excellent mistakes, their learnings and their ways forward. You are the most helpful person do discover the ways you can grow you.

Spontaneous

Some persons have fun growing forward one of the twelve with a spontaneous spirit of exploring and innovating. Select one of the twelve learnings. Spontaneously, practice this one possibility, this one best practice, for *this one day.*

Whichever possibility, whichever best practice you choose to do, the primary focus is on the spontaneous nature of the practice. Sometimes, we spontaneously sing a tune that stirs our spirit. Sometimes, we spontaneously run—with a spirit of joy for being alive. Sometimes, we share a spontaneous act of kindness.

The art is to do this best practice, keeping the spontaneous spirit of the learning. We are not trying to practice this learning in a humdrum, monotonous manner. We share our practice with a fresh, open, spirit of wonder and joy, creativity and imagination.

One Day

In both the AA and Al-A-Non movements, the best practice is to give up drinking *one day at a time.* The goal is not to give up drinking forever, permanently, or for ten years, or for even a year. The encouragement is that the person can give up drinking for *one day at a time.* Likewise, as one grows forward a constructive life of grace, one can do a best practice of a productive behavior of grace for *one day at a time.*

The art is to practice a helpful learning for one day. The art is to relax, have fun, enjoy life, and live in the grace of God, for this one day. The art is not to be tense and tight, nervous and anxious, enslaved to a compulsive, addictive perfectionism. Grace is encouraging and hopeful, realistic and achievable, invitational and inspiring.

Week End

For many people, a week end is an opportunity to practice one of the twelve learnings of grace. The week end is sufficiently open and uncluttered that they can "exercise" their learning of grace on the week end. For many, the week end is a "project time." Select a specific learning as your project for a specific week end.

Frequently, you can match the week end and the learning. For example, you can decide to practice the third learning, "have fun." This matches with how you plan to invest your time on the week end. You might decide to practice the seventh learning, "let go." The art is to think of the helpful use of the week end and which best practice would be fun to explore.

Work Week

For some persons, a work week is five days, or six days. It varies from one person to the next. For some, the work week is seven days. Yes, and for some, the work week is four days, albeit ten hour days. You might decide to select a specific work week and practice a specific learning for that one work week.

Given the rhythm of your work weeks, you might select a specific work week in September and decide to practice the fifth learning, "build on your strengths." For another specific work week, say in December, you might select the eighth learning, "compassion runs." The art is to think of the flow of your work and consider which learning you would have fun exploring and practicing for that one specific work week.

You are not trying to shift from a daily to a weekly pattern of growing forward. You are simply, for one specific week, seeking to grow forward. You want to keep all eight best practices open to you. There is no merit in a weekly pattern over any of the other seven ways.

Whole Week

I encourage you to select a specific whole week. Do not think of a whole week as though you were going to grow forward your learnings and experiences of grace in "whole week" ways for the whole of the coming year. Be very specific. Select a given week. You might select the week before Easter, or the week before Christmas. You might select the week of July 4th, or the third week in September, or the week of your birthday or anniversary.

You are not trying to "expand" to the length of a whole week, as though you are now going to focus your growing in "whole week" ways. You are simply going to grow your learnings forward for one specific whole week.

Twelve Days

Some persons have fun discovering these twelve learnings as "Twelve Days of Best Practices." People do this in the twelve days before Christmas, the twelve days before Easter, or the twelve days at the beginning of September. This is like a beginning exploration and orientation of the twelve learnings to discover which, for you, are:

- Natural and easy
- A little more advanced
- Advanced
- Difficult

You can do these twelve learnings in whatever order you discover is helpful for you. You are welcome to have fun doing these "Twelve Days of Best Practices." These are twelve ways you can live in the grace of God. Practice one learning a day for twelve days as best practices. Feel free, for twelve days, to have fun, live in the grace of God, and give thanks to God.

Deepen your experiences of living in the grace of God. *This day,* as you look to the day before you, say to yourself, or, better yet, say out loud, the learning, the best practice, you plan to live for *this one day.* Live these learnings, these possibilities, these best practices, one day at a time, for twelve days.

Twelve Days of Best Practices

1. Today, I live my compassion.	Today, I live in the grace of God.	I give thanks to God.
2. Today, I claim my strengths.	Today, I live in the grace of God.	I give thanks to God.
3. Today, I build on my strengths.	Today, I live in the grace of God.	I give thanks to God.
4. Today, I value excellent mistakes.	Today, I live in the grace of God.	I give thanks to God.
5. Today, I live progress.	Today, I live in the grace of God.	I give thanks to God.
6. Today, I have fun.	Today, I live in the grace of God.	I give thanks to God.
7. Today, I let go.	Today, I live in the grace of God.	I give thanks to God.
8. Today, I run with compassion.	Today, I live in the grace of God.	I give thanks to God.
9. Today, I live humility and wisdom.	Today, I live in the grace of God.	I give thanks to God.
10. Today, I share just enough help.	Today, I live in the grace of God.	I give thanks to God.
11. Today, I live two for one	Today, I live in the grace of God.	I give thanks to God.
12. Today, I live hope.	Today, I live in the grace of God.	I give thanks to God.

Some persons post these twelve learnings on their refrigerator, on their bathroom mirror, on their calendar, on their cell phone, or as a screen saver on their computer. They do so with the spirit of having fun, growing their life forward, *this day, today.*

Having done twelve days of best practices, you will have a sense of which three learnings are natural and easy for you. You can decide to focus on these three for a period of time. You will sense when these are so much a part of whom you are that you can move on to a new three.

Or, you can select a new twelve days. You can have fun doing the twelve learnings in a new sequence, a new rhythm, with a new tune. Select a new, fun order for these learnings you would have fun exploring and discovering, deepening and strengthening in your life.

Or, you can practice some of these twelve learnings with a spontaneous, *one day at a time* spirit, having fun with now this one—and now this one—and now this one, in a free flowing, encouraging, and exploring spirit.

Monthly

Many persons have fun discovering these twelve learnings as monthly best practices. They select one learning as their focus for a given month. They have fun developing their competencies for this one learning during the given month.

They may or may not practice this one learning for each day of the given month. The focus is on the one learning for the month, even as the one learning may, now here, now there, on this day, or that day, be practiced during the month.

The spirit is one of wonder and joy, creativity and imagination, not routine and drudgery, chore and toil. You can think of the monthly pattern in this way:

Live your compassion	December
Claim your strengths	January
Have fun	February
Value excellent mistakes	March
Build on your strengths	April
Live progress	May
Let go	June
Compassion runs	July

Humility and wisdom	August
Just enough help	September
Two for one	October
Live hope	November

During each month, you can focus on one of the twelve learnings. This can be your "lectionary for learning." This can be your focus for each of twelve months. You can grow forward your gifts, strengths, and competencies—one month at a time. You can experience the grace of God. You can live with gratitude.

Seasonal

For many persons, a seasonal pattern of growing forward is helpful. Seasons vary for persons, depending on their common interests and life stages. For many, the seasons of spring, summer, fall, and winter are important. For many, the season of being in a warm climate during six months of the year and being "back home, up north" are the two major seasons of the year.

For many who are in school, the seasons have something to do with fall semester, spring semester, and summer work or school. For many, the four seasons are football, basketball, soccer, and baseball. For many, the seasons have something to do with planting, growing, harvesting, and fallow seasons. For many, the seasons have to do with fishing, harvesting, repairing nets and boats, and land chores.

There are distinctive seasons for different stages of life. With small children, the seasons have something to do with the school year. With young men and young women in college, the seasons have to do with semesters and spring breaks. With retired persons, the seasons may have to do with a season of winter in the south, and a season of summer in the north.

You will know the seasons that are important for you, for this time in your life.

For some persons, whose seasons are fall, winter, spring, and summer, their best practices might look like:

Fall	The season of compassion
Winter	The season of strengths
Spring	The season of humility and wisdom
Summer	The season of fun

Select any four best practices, best learnings, and focus on each for a season. The next year—the next four seasons—select another four and grow forward your own learnings of these best practices.

Yes, you can select one of the twelve learnings and practice this learning for a season. You can practice another learning during yet another season. Across the seasons important in your life, you can focus on one learning during each season. God will bless you. You will experience the grace of God. You will give thanks to God.

All eight ways, all eight best practices are available to you. There is no one way for everyone to grow forward in living a life in grace. And, yes, you can select any of these eight ways, these eight best practices, to grow forward your learnings and experiences of grace.

CREATIVITY AND STABILITY

The grace of God is creative and improvisational, making all things new. The grace of God is regular and customary, stable and enduring. Feel free to grow forward your experiences of the grace of God with creativity - in creative, improvisational ways. Feel free to grow forward your experiences of the grace of God with stability - in regular, customary ways.

Feel free to *not* grow forward your experiences of the grace of God in *only* regular, customary ways. When you are creative and improvisational in growing forward your learnings of grace, you match with the creative and improvisational nature of grace.

When you are only routine and customary, you miss a major resource for experiencing the nature, the richness, and the joy of grace.

We do not control the grace of God.

God's grace comes to us in ways we do not anticipate. The grace of God comes to us—now here, now there—in creative, improvisational ways.

Yes, the grace of God is fully present in our lives, stable and enduring, regular and customary, in each moment of each hour of each day. And, with surprising freshness and newness, the grace of God touches our lives with amazing creativity and originality, with improvisation and innovation.

Thus, keep yourself open to both the improvisational creativity and the regular, customary experiences of God's grace in your life. Further, grow forward some of these twelve learnings in both improvisational ways and in regular ways.

Vary your learnings. Vary the ways in which you learn. Live your compassion. Claim your strengths. Have fun.

Do not try to perfect all twelve. See the twelve as possibilities, as learnings, as best practices. The goal is not to have all twelve. The goal is to live in the grace of God. Persons who experience *some* of these twelve learnings live in the grace of God.

Give yourself the freedom to live with a sense of grace and adventure, good fun and compassion. Feel free to share your creativity and flexibility with yourself. Feel free to share your compassion with yourself. Feel free to share your compassion with your family, your friends, and the persons God gives you.

Feel free to grow forward, living in the grace of God.

III

The Blessing

GOD BLESS YOU

GRACE AND LIFE

Grace and life are good friends. Grace stirs life. Life encourages grace.

The grace of God is the beginning of life. Earth, moon, sun, stars—Milky Way, star clusters and galaxies, big clouds and dark holes, nearby planets and outer solar systems, new stars and giant stars, gas and dust swirls, solar winds and interstellar winds—all these are gifts of the grace of God.

These are not the result of some dark force, unknowing and unknowable. These elements of the universe stir and thrive, exist and move forward as gifts of the grace of God. The life of the universe, with its swirlings and stirrings, is the gift of the grace of God. The beginnings and stirrings of life are through God's grace.

You—we—are alive through the grace of God. Our being born is the gift of the grace of God. We are blessed with gifts, strengths, and competencies through the grace of God. We live and move, love and think, discover compassion, community, hope, wisdom and judgment, creativity and common sense through the grace of God.

Grace stirs life. Life encourages grace. Wherever we discover life, we discover grace. Grace is drawn to life. Grace yearns for life. Life attracts grace. There is something about life that is alluring to grace. When we are our most alive, we sense the rich, full presence of grace.

GRACE AND PEACE

God blesses you with grace and peace, comfort and joy, happiness and hope. Indeed, God does bless you with grace and peace. Likewise, you are free to bless yourself with grace and peace. Sometimes, you and I get in the way of God's blessings of grace and peace. Sometimes, you and I are our own "worst enemy."

We become so preoccupied with the busyness and hurriedness of life that we do not allow the grace and peace of God to fully surround us, lead us, and bless us. We think more poorly of ourselves than we have a right to. We allow distractions and deceits to lead us astray. We look down on ourselves. We think too highly of ourselves. We overcompensate for thinking too poorly of ourselves. We move from one extreme to the other.

Grace and peace are good friends. Grace brings peace. Peace brings grace. The two gifts bless our lives. We have the confidence that the grace of God blesses us. We have the assurance that the peace of God gives us a wonderful life of wonder and joy, compassion and wisdom, comfort and hope. God blesses us. We bless ourselves. We do not think too poorly nor too highly of ourselves. We bless ourselves because God blesses us.

These twelve learnings help us to live with balance and integrity, with confidence and assurance. We grow forward our life with fullness and richness, with grace and peace. God blesses you. Feel free to bless yourself—to accept God's blessings—to honor God's blessings—and to live with grace and peace.

Let your life be a parable of grace.

Live the grace and peace and hope God gives you.

God bless you with grace and peace. Amen.

Prayer

May the grace of God be with you,
May the compassion of Christ surround you,
May the hope of the Holy Spirit lead you.
God bless you with grace and peace.

Amen.

IV

Author, Books,

Appreciation

Author

KENNON L. CALLAHAN, PH. D.

Kennon L. Callahan - author, researcher, professor, theologian, and pastor - is a number one bestselling author and among today's most sought-after speakers and consultants.

Dr. Callahan's newest and nineteenth book is **Living in Grace**.

He has worked with thousands of groupings around the world and has helped tens of thousands of persons and leaders. His helpful seminars are filled with encouragement, compassion, wisdom, and practical possibilities.

Dr. Callahan's research travels have led him to all of the states in the United States, all of the provinces in Canada, the Arctic, Norway, Holland, England, Denmark, Sweden, Finland, Estonia, Germany, Russia, Turkey, Greece, Italy, Spain, France, Egypt, Lebanon, Palestine, Jordan, Israel, Mexico, the British Virgin Islands, the Bahamas, Chile, Brazil, and the Antarctica. His current research interests are in both cultural archaeology and in human behavior.

Author of many books, he is best known for his groundbreaking **Twelve Keys to an Effective Church**, which has formed the basis for the widely acclaimed Mission Growth Movement, which is helping many persons across the planet.

Dr. Callahan has earned B. A., M. Div., S. T. M., and Ph. D. degrees.

He has served as a pastor of rural and city congregations in Ohio, Texas, and Georgia.

He taught for many years at Emory University.

His three recent books include the new edition of **Twelve Keys to an Effective Church,** the new edition of the **Twelve Keys Leaders' Guide,** and the new **Twelve Keys Bible Study.** Altogether, he is the author of nineteen books.

Ken and Julie, his wife, celebrated being married for fifty six years on August 11, 2012. They have two sons, Ken, Jr., and Michael, and three grandsons: Blake, Mason, and Brice. They enjoy being with their family and their many good friends. They share good fun and good times with the outdoors, hiking, camping, reading, researching, traveling, quilting, and sailing.

Ken and Julie Callahan are visiting friends in the Shenandoah Valley of Virginia, enjoying the Blue Ridge Mountains with the Skyline Drive meandering along the ridges.

The picture is taken at the Rivers Bend Ranch of Elaine and Mac McConnell, outside of Stanley, Virginia. Ken and Julie are on the deck of Richard and Elizabeth Worden's Avion travel trailer on the Ranch.

Richard Worden, their long time, good friend, is taking the picture. Richard has written of Ken and Julie, "The history and beauty of the Valley grace their lives even as they have graced the lives of friends, colleagues and congregations for decades."

BOOKS BY KENNON L. CALLAHAN, PH.D.

Living in Grace

This is a joyful, encouraging book that shares possibilities for living in grace. You will discover twelve decisive events. Each event will strengthen your living in grace. These events and their learnings have helped many persons to live whole, healthy lives in the grace of God. You will find this book helpful in your own life—living in grace.

Twelve Keys to an Effective Church: Strong, Healthy Congregations Living in the Grace of God, Second Edition
ISBN 978-0-470-55929-1

For the first time in print, the five basic qualities for strong, healthy congregations. New possibilities for the *Twelve Keys* to an effective, successful congregation. New suggestions for expanding your current strengths and adding new strengths. New wisdom and insights on mission, sacrament, and grace. The book helps you to be a mission growth congregation.

The Twelve Keys Leaders' Guide: An Approach for Grassroots, Key Leaders, and Pastors Together ISBN 978-0-470-55928-4

The book helps you lead your congregation in developing a strong, healthy future. It shares excellent ideas and good suggestions on how to lead a helpful *Twelve Keys* planning retreat. The book provides resources for encouraging action, implementation, and momentum. It shares insights on the dynamics of memory, change, conflict, and hope in congregations. It is an excellent companion for the new *Twelve Keys* book.

The Twelve Keys Bible Study ISBN 978-0-470-55916-1 The book shares the biblical resources for the *Twelve Keys*. It shares scriptures for each of the *Twelve Keys* and reflections on these scriptures. It shares suggestions and questions for study and conversation. This resource is helpful for Advent and Lenten Bible studies, and for preaching and worship services. The book is an excellent companion Bible study for the new *Twelve Keys* book.

The Future That Has Come ISBN 0 7879 49817

The seven major paradigm shifts of recent years. New possibilities for reaching and growing the grassroots. Motivating and leading your congregation.

Small, Strong Congregations   ISBN 0 7879 49809

Ministers, leaders, and members of small congregations develop a strong, healthy future together.

A New Beginning for Pastors and Congregations ISBN 0 7879 42898

What to do in the first three months of a new pastorate; how to make a new start in a present pastorate.

Preaching Grace   ISBN 0 7879 42952

Pastors develop an approach to preaching that matches their own distinctive gifts. Their preaching shares the spirit of grace with their people,

Twelve Keys for Living   ISBN 0 7879 41409

People claim the strengths God gives them and develop a whole, healthy life. Solid Lenten or Advent study.

Visiting in an Age of Mission   ISBN 0 7879 38688

Develop shepherding in your congregation. Groupings to shepherd. The variety of ways you can do so.

Effective Church Finances ISBN 0 7879 38696

Develop an effective budget, set solid giving goals, and increase the giving of your congregation.

Dynamic Worship ISBN 0 7879 38661

Major resources for stirring, inspiring worship services, helpful and hopeful in advancing people's lives.

Giving and Stewardship ISBN 0 7879 3867X

How to grow generous givers. Motivations out of which people give. Six primary sources of giving. Giving principles in generous congregations. How to encourage your whole giving family.

Effective Church Leadership ISBN 0 7879 38653

Foundational life searches. Seven best ways to grow leaders. Develop constructive leadership.

Building for Effective Mission ISBN 0 7879 38726

Develop your mission. Evaluate locations. Maximize current facilities. Building new space.

Create an effective building team. Selecting an architect. Develop an extraordinary first year.

Twelve Keys to an Effective Church ISBN 0 7879 38718

Claim your current strengths, expand some, and add new strengths to be a strong, healthy congregation. Encourage your whole congregation to study this book—it helps in their church, family, work, and life.

Twelve Keys: The Planning Workbook ISBN 0 7879 38734

Each person contributes directly to creating an effective long-range plan for your future together.

Twelve Keys: The Leaders' Guide ISBN 0 7879 3870x

How to lead your congregation in developing an effective plan for your future. How to develop action, implementation, and momentum. Dealing with the dynamics of memory, change, conflict, and hope.

Twelve Keys: The Study Guide ISBN 0 7879 39420

An excellent Bible study of the *Twelve Keys,* with helpful resources and solid discussion possibilities.

WORDS OF APPRECIATION

I am most grateful to these persons for their wisdom,
their encouragement, and their helpful contributions
to *Living in Grace*.

DORIS HOFFMAN

I want to thank Doris Jean Hoffman for serving as editor of this
work. Her encouraging spirit, her wisdom, and her
precision of focus have made this monograph an even
more helpful and insightful work.

I am grateful to her for sharing many excellent ideas and
good suggestions. Our conversations together have been most
helpful. Doris has a deep love for life, ministry, and music. She
brings much wisdom and experience for the benefit of this work.

I am humbly thankful for her amazing gifts. She is an extraordinary person. She has helped me in developing this helpful and
historic work. Across the years, I have shared and worked with
many persons. Her contributions stand among the very best.

Doris was born and grew up in Cuyahoga Falls, Ohio.
She and Julie Callahan, my wife, are cousins, growing up in the same
town. Doris's father and Julie's mother were brother and sister. Their

common originating name is Ross. Doris had a distinguished career in the service of her country: First, for fourteen years in the intelligence branch of Sandia National Laboratories in Albuquerque, New Mexico, where she received exceptional and unusual training in all areas of security, and earned numerous awards for her own innovative concepts and leadership abilities.

In 1996 she was offered and accepted a position in the newly formed Clandestine Information Technology Office at the headquarters of the Central Intelligence Agency, in Langley, Virginia. She retired with honors from the CIA in 2001.

For forty-three years Doris directed children's choirs, recently assuming a well-deserved "retirement". She has herself been singing in choirs non-stop for seventy years (beginning alongside this author at the age of five) and is active in the Chancel Choir of St. John's United Methodist Church of Aiken, South Carolina, where she also serves as a Stephen Minister. Volunteering throughout the community is her most enjoyable way of life in retirement.

SARA HURON

I want to thank Sara Huron for serving as contributing editor of this work. Sara brings remarkable competencies to the development of this work. Her compassion and wisdom are unsurpassed.

She has an encouraging spirit and her capacity for gently coaching persons to their best strengths is outstanding.

Her ability to give leadership to a group of people, whether in a large business firm or in a volunteer grouping, is extraordinary.

Sara shares her compassion, grace, and wisdom through her firm, Wide Margins. She offers help and hope to those God gives her through consulting, coaching, and spiritual direction. What people thank her most for are her gifts of careful listening, wise counsel, and presence.

RICHARD WORDEN

I want to thank Richard Worden, born in Pikeville, Kentucky, deep in the mountains of Appalachia. Richard was educated first grade through freshman college year at the Training School and Academy of Pikeville College, founded by the Presbyterian Church.

Little did he realize at the time the treasure of the sound biblical foundation those Presbyterians would provide that Methodist boy. While in Speed Scientific School, University of Louisville, aiming toward a career as an engineer, he responded to the call to the ministry.

After graduating from Kentucky Wesleyan College in Owensboro Kentucky, he married the love of his life, Elizabeth Reeves Gamble. They started their life together in Gilbert Hall apartments, Candler School of Theology, Emory University.

Richard served forty-one years in the Virginia Conference, leading four congregations. He was the founding pastor of St. Stephen's in Northern Virginia, pastor of South Roanoke, senior pastor of Annandale and Reveille congregations and superintendent of the Alexandria and Roanoke Districts.

There are many grace points in Richard's life. They include the special relationships a pastor shares with the people he serves and leading congregations forward in mission. Midpoint in his career Richard met Ken Callahan. In classes, at consultations in local churches, through a growing friendship, Ken has been one of those grace points. He has also been a good travel companion. Together, they have traveled to the Mediterranean, the Baltic, the Antarctic and the Arctic regions.

Through their fifty-five years of marriage, Richard has had the loving and strong support of Elizabeth. They are unusually blessed with a vibrant family life. Their three daughters and their husbands, three granddaughters and five grandsons bring astounding blessings of grace to them. Richard and Elizabeth affirm the joy of "living in grace".

LEO BARDES

I want to thank Leo Bardes. Leo was born in 1931 in Calistoga, California, in the heart of the wine country. His parents were Greek immigrants. They had a son and a daughter.

In 1952, he earned an AA degree from Santa Rosa Junior College, and then a BA degree in music from San Francisco State University. During the Korean conflict, he served in the Second Army Band, stationed near Washington, DC – the only US Army band to have a Bag Pipe Corp. attached to it. While in the service, he married Sylvia Jackson. They have two children.

He went back to S F State University to earn a MA degree.

He spent 8 years teaching music in St. Helena, CA. The high point there was when his high school band was chosen to be part of the opening ceremonies for the Winter Olympic Games at Squaw Valley, CA.

In 1965, he left to become Band Director at the College of San Mateo – a large community college on the San Francisco Peninsula. They lived near Portola Valley in the foothills behind Stanford University.

At the College of San Mateo, he served as a classroom instructor, Music Department Chairman, then Dean of Creative Arts, a member of the Chancellor's staff, then as Vice President of Instruction. His last year was capped by being both VP and Acting President during the President's vacation.

He also served as choir director for several Peninsula churches and as a clinician/judge for High School and Junior High Band Festivals. He retired in 1992.

In 2000, they moved to Medford, Oregon. His hobbies are being a member of a monthly book club, playing golf, fly fishing and writing poetry.

Made in the USA
San Bernardino, CA
19 February 2013